Your Home Is Your Castle

Your Home Is Your Castle:

Live Like an A-Lister in a Post Pandemic World

By
Nelson Aspen

RED SKY PRESENTS
NEW YORK

Cover design and interior page layout by Jesse Sanchez
www.jsanchezart.com

Edited by Charlene Keel

Photography by Garrett Rowland

To Jonny, the Prince in our Castle.

And to Mother, who was Everything.

———————

Table of Contents:

About the Author

Nelson Aspen has enjoyed a long career in television first as an actor, then a reporter and then two decades as the Entertainment Editor for Australia's top-rated morning program, Sunrise. The 2020 recipient of the Publicists Guild of America's distinguished International Media Award, he has covered myriad stories and events (from Oscars' red-carpets to arrests and deaths to marriages and milestones of the biggest names in pop culture) and interviewed hundreds of A-List celebrities on a wide range of subjects. He is your "One Degree of Separation" from all things Showbiz!

The author of five previous books and veteran of twenty marathons, Nelson is also a popular cabaret star and has performed his one-man shows all around the globe from Broadway and Hollywood to London's West End, international music festivals and the famed Sydney Opera House. When he isn't working, running or singing, he is devoted to making a happy home in Harlem, NYC, with his partner Jonny.

The Welcome Mat

——————

I am a New Yorker. You don't have to be born and raised in the Empire State to be a real New Yorker, but you do have to be tough, resilient and open-minded. From my adolescence in rural Pennsylvania, I somehow knew that New York (specifically Manhattan) was my "true north" so as soon as I finished school, I fled to the Big Apple. I was nineteen years old and lived with a roommate in a roach-infested flat smack dab in the center of Hell's Kitchen on the same block as several Broadway Theaters, a strip club, a cabaret lounge and a transvestite hooker bar. Hooker, not hookah.

In real estate, they say it's all about "Location, location, location!" And that grimy, gritty first home was perfectly situated for my entry into an independent adulthood. As the years went on, I moved to "better" neighborhoods, but always happily learned to make "home" in every new apartment, regardless of its urban limitations. I found a mentor in Emmy winning Daytime Television acting royalty, Mary Stuart (*Search for Tomorrow, Guiding Light*), who paid me for my secretarial services with acting lessons and life coaching—although that phrase had yet to be coined. She lived in an elegant but unpretentious pre-war penthouse apartment on the corner of Madison Avenue and 68th Street. I spent tons of time there and learned much from Mary's natural sense of style and graciousness. Her knack for mixing martinis, feeding the homeless, writing,

thank you notes, pet care and concocting the perfect omelets all became part of my routine skill set.

"Blooming wherever I'm planted" continued when I relocated to Los Angeles to pursue my broadcast career. I started out on a friend's sofa bed and eventually progressed to a roommate situation before renting my own studio apartment. Living in LA has all the same challenges as any city, but at least there is plenty of sunshine. Maybe too much nice weather. Unless there is a milestone event, like an earthquake, the years have a way of slipping by without any clear-cut seasons to delineate the passage of time. My apartments got bigger until I was renting a house and then, in 1997, bought my first property. My TV career had finally taken off and the charming bungalow I'd nicknamed "the Hollywood Ha-Hacienda" became a laboratory for me to experiment with lifestyle ideas, design and party planning. I wrote books and contributed to many news and talk shows as part of the burgeoning "How To" trend of the late 1990s. One day I was demonstrating ideas for throwing an Oscar party (Leonardo Di-Cappucino, anyone?) and the next I was mixing mocktails for your kids' Prom Parties. Somewhere in there I also became a fitness expert and was commissioned to train Princess Diana in that "hot, new workout craze," Step Aerobics and started interviewing every celebrity in Tinseltown for myriad morning television shows. In fact, demonstrating the Princess' workout on British breakfast TV was the baptism of my now decades-long tenure as a televised Dawn Patroller.

A breaking news assignment in 2008 ended up dramatically changing the California lifestyle to which I'd become so accustomed. I was actually in Bermuda to run a marathon and spend some alone time working on a book when the news broke that actor Heath Ledger had died unexpectedly in New York City, from an accidental overdose. My Executive Producer ordered me off the tropical island immediately: "Get the next plane to New York!" It was January 22 (deep-freeze time in NYC), so I had to buy a winter wardrobe at the airport as soon as I landed at JFK—and then I spent the next several days in front of Heath's SoHo residence, somberly reporting the developments of his demise as they unfolded.

Even under such sad circumstances and meteorologically challenging conditions, New York City started to seduce me again, like an old flame. I started taking on whatever assignments I could find to justify being back in my former "hometown" and reconnecting with my oldest and dearest friends and family members. I pushed the button and bought a small pied a terre and began commuting between the East and West Coasts, two weeks at a time. I joked that I'd become Bi-Coastal, since Bi-Sexual hadn't worked out very well for me!

I soon found that every fortnight when I was crossing the RFK Bridge to head to the airport and fly back to California, I was already homesick for my little slice of Manhattan. So, in 2012, I finally sold the Ha-Hacienda and came home. Twenty-two years in LA? You get less time for murder!

My 350-square-foot studio had been the perfect city crash pad, but it would be too tiny for a full-time residence. And the quaint, roomy digs you see on *Friends* and *Sex and the City* are far more unrealistic than any of the storylines. Pure fiction! (If I were to point to a TV set that best depicts an "average" NYC apartment, it's probably Jerry Seinfeld's).

Luckily, I bellied up to the bar at one of my favorite local bistros, Cafe Luxembourg, where I struck up a conversation with a real estate broker and told him of my plight. He was certain he had the perfect place for me and, even though I was skeptical about venturing outside my neighborhood comfort zone, I agreed to take a look and (to my happy surprise) he was right. It was a wonderful, still-small (500 square feet) apartment on a picturesque block (84th Street) on Manhattan's Upper West Side, just off Riverside Park. It's known as "Edgar Allan Poe Street" because the author once lived in a farmhouse there. The first neighbor to welcome me, amazingly, was none other than showbiz icon Jerry Stiller, who lived a few doors down with his wife and comedy partner, Anne, was a great omen of happy times ahead. Life in my home base was sweet for nine years, while I broadcasted daily and traveled the world on exciting work assignments. My penchant for Entertaining and Home projects flourished and I wrote two more books on the subject. Just in time for my fiftieth birthday in 2013, inspired by the lavish party my best friend threw for me in his stunning Hamptons home, I was asked to pen a manual for "living well in Middle Age." It would turn out that I was only just getting started. For me, Life really began at fifty!

Just as 2014 arrived, so did the most unexpected gift of all: I met my life partner, Jonny. I was an avowed bachelor with a personal motto of being "alone but not lonely" so all the cliches about finding love when you're not looking for it ring completely true for me. The biggest adventure of all for us is the fact that, although he had a beautiful apartment right up the street from mine, he works in Hong Kong. So began our jet-setting, multicontinental relationship, seeing each other every few weeks somewhere one or both of us could continue working. I began taking on concert gigs (yes, I am a singer) to help facilitate more travel. In 2019 alone, I made twenty-nine trips! We really gave our passports a workout as we rendezvoused in locales from Singapore to Sydney, from Napa Valley to French Polynesia! I called ours "a relationship of honeymoons."

We were closer than ever and decided the time had come to finally create a home-base, together. Given where we were on the chronological spectrum of life, "the time" also dictated that it should indeed be our dream home . . . with all the amenities, bells and whistles we could afford. Then, in another decade or so, when we would start to look toward eventual retirement, we could downsize or simply our lifestyle.

There was no question about remaining on Manhattan's Upper West Side, close to Jonny's beloved alma mater, Columbia University, and all our favorite parks, museums, markets, restaurants and theaters. Over the years, I'd inched my way northward from 45th Street to 69th . . . to 84th . . . to 108th, always seeking to experience the original spirit of what makes a NYC neighborhood so unique. Other requirements included the security and convenience of a 24-hour-attended lobby and doorman, a gym, a live-in superintendent, and some private outdoor space. Most of the floorplans we liked were three-bedroom units with one bedroom that could be absorbed into the main living area and a second bedroom to convert into a combination office and TV studio. Our real estate agent strived to show us what was available, but the only place that mutually excited us would all but completely drain our bank accounts and the owners weren't keen on negotiating. Fortunately, we were not in a rush.

One morning shortly after four, unable to sleep, I surrendered to the siren call of social media. As I scrolled through my Instagram feed, up popped an advertisement for a new luxury condominium complex under construction in nearby historic Harlem. By four-thirty, I was sitting up in bed, combing through every bit of information I could find about the building and the surrounding area. By five a.m., I'd emailed and left a voicemail for their sponsor's representative and by nine a.m. I was standing outside their model unit around the corner from the construction site. Sara DiMaggio greeted me with a firm handshake, a hot coffee and a personality that could "sell an igloo to an Eskimo!" An hour after seeing the model unit and several floorplans that fit our criteria, I was on the phone to Hong Kong, telling Jonny we would be donning hard hats and visiting the construction site as soon as he could schedule a flight back to NYC.

Even in its skeletal stage, the building looked glorious. We toured several apartments and, even without walls and only concrete slabs, it was love at first sight. We spent the rest of the day wandering around, exploring the environs, from the famed Apollo Theater to the West Harlem Piers and Red Rooster restaurant. Morningside Park, rows and rows of immaculate brownstone townhomes, art galleries and the magnificent churches and campus of City College charmed us. It was time to crunch the numbers. There is a song in my cabaret repertoire, *Love in a Home* from the 1956

Broadway musical *Li'l Abner* (Music by Gene DePaul and lyrics by the great Johnny Mercer). As a housewarming gift, I used to belt it out for our friends whenever they'd move into a new place — before the furniture arrived and the acoustics really allowed me to let it rip, loud and powerfully! The melody is sweet and simple (search for it sometime on YouTube) and the lyrics are meaningful:

You can tell,
When you open the door!
You can tell,
When there's love in a home!
Every table and chair seem to smile,
Come on in, sit a spell, stay a while.
You almost feel you've been there once before,
By the shine and the glow of the room!
And the clock seems to chime,
Come again anytime,
You'll be welcome wherever you roam!
You can tell when there's love in a home!

That song not only sprang to mind while we were touring the building, it stayed in my head the rest of the entire day. While I may not necessarily believe in omens, I do believe in simpatico. And I do believe it's one thing to buy a house — it's quite another to make it a home. And "home" is exactly the vibe we both got from this Harlem hideaway. You know when it's time to follow your instincts. Gut feelings aren't to be dismissed.

That night, sitting on bar stools at one of our local favorites, Coppola's Italian Restaurant on West 79th Street, we poured over the offering plan while we drank chianti and devoured lasagna.

"Let's go for it," I said.

"Better yet, let's spring for the Penthouse!" Jonny replied.

The Penthouse! I was gobsmacked! I vowed to make it our Harlem Ha-Hacienda.

In an ironic twist, it soon dawned on me that my much loved and missed mentor, Mary Stuart, had been exactly fifty-seven when we began our special relationship back in the 1980s: the same age I was at that moment at Coppola's. Fifty-seven was really a "prime time" for her: enjoying a long, esteemed career in TV, success as both an author and singer, a healthy, committed relationship with a partner she adored . . . and a dream home in the form of a sprawling Manhattan penthouse in the sky.

"Ticking the boxes" of the very same life goals she had inspired me to set for myself was coming to fruition. I couldn't blow it now! With that in mind, I wanted to compile this book to inspire others to feel empowered and to create their own dream homes, regardless of where they live, what they earn, or what stage of life they're in. As we evolve, so do our perceptions of what a "dream home" would be.

An informal, and highly UN-scientific, poll I posted to Instagram asked, "Do you live in your dream home?" After thousands of votes were cast, the results showed that 71% felt they were NOT living in their dream. Even if you're one of the fortunate 29%, your ideals and priorities will almost certainly evolve and change. So, too, can your environs. Don't be afraid of this . . . embrace it. Invest in it. Not necessarily for the investment of the property itself, but for the value of your personal happiness and fulfillment. In another random poll, I asked if folks would rather move into a ready-made Dream Home, or design theirs from scratch. It was an almost exact even split with "from scratch" only squeaking ahead at fifty-one percent.

So, whether you're going for Move-In Ready or tackling the ultimate domestic project, more than ever in modern history your home should be your castle, and you deserve to feel like royalty when you're there. It is where you will be making lifelong memories. I hope in the pages that follow you'll find helpful inspiration and instruction to help achieve that marvelous sense of satisfaction and wellbeing. Feel free to jump around these pages, mark them up and make notes in the margins. Any useful tidbit could make all the difference for your domestic bliss!

Tackling the Hunt

———————

The penthouse we initially put an offer on was not the unit we ended up with and we were lucky to be able to make the swap while we could. The first unit had some fetching architectural features, including a winding staircase up to a private rooftop cabana with 180-degree views stretching from the Hudson River to the East River. We signed contracts, donned our hard hats, and rode the elevator back up to survey our new spread. We had worked with the property developer to alter the floorplans pre-construction so as not to build the "second bedroom." Instead, we would incorporate it into the main living area to make one grand room with a dining alcove. But as we stood behind the tarp and netting where the actual exterior walls would be built, we gazed out to the neighboring, unsold unit. It had an expansive terrace adjoining both the living room and main bedroom—overlooking the famed Apollo Theater marquee. FOMO (Fear of Missing Out) washed over us. We didn't have a terrace!

The contractors and real estate agent took us next door to see this apartment and, while it didn't have the interior stairway to the rooftop cabana, it had a much larger laundry room, wider showers, higher ceilings and that breathtaking terrace (actually larger in square footage than the main bedroom). With floor to ceiling windows throughout, the added terrace would visually enhance the spacious look of the place and we

could landscape and decorate it to make it feel like an extension of the unit itself. While our personal cabana would need to be accessed by the building's main elevator or corridor stairwell, we immediately realized we would get far more use and daily pleasure out of the terrace. Sunrise coffee in the morning, sunset cocktails in the evening! Fortunately, we were able to make an even swap so never underestimate the positive role that Serendipity can play in your search for a Dream Home (Remember the pop-up Instagram ad that alerted me to the property in the first place!).

Some homes, for the sake of open space, seem to assault you with everything, all at once, from the time you enter. Wham! Kitchen, living, dining spaces all in one. This can be especially true in apartments, so we were conscientious about delineating these areas with corners and a structural pillar. From the foyer you can turn left to the kitchen or right to the bedroom. Around the corner is the dining alcove and through a vestibule you can access the office, a bathroom and laundry room. You don't need a ton of square footage to make a "West Wing" and an "East Wing."

We could have saved ourselves incalculable time, effort and money if Jonny and I had simply decided to move in together into one of the homes we already owned, but I never wanted either of us to feel like we were living in the other's space. After seven years together, it was time to create something that was mutually ours, without having to acclimatize to someone else's orbit. That works for many couples, either by happenstance or need, but we were two guys in their mid-fifties . . . with different tastes and different collections of art, memorabilia and assorted treasures. Merging our personal lives had been easy. Combining our physical, domestic ones was a challenge to be met. It also required we be judicious, cooperative, patient and open to professional assistance whenever possible. Dogs and kids: two kinds of co-stars W.C. Fields famously avoided. Although we (especially Jonny) love both canines and kinder, we don't have either but wanted to find a property that would be pet/child friendly. Especially after living through a pandemic, people know how vital it is that everyone can co-exist and thrive comfortably whether it's for remote learning, working from home or bunkering down for quarantine.

One of my closest friends and cabaret co-stars, showbiz legend Anita Gillette (most famous as Miss Mona in the movie Moonstruck, Tina Fey's mom on 30 Rock and a slew of Broadway shows) continues to enjoy a fifty-plus year career with Manhattan as her home base—all while having raised her kids in the confines of the city. I asked her the key to juggling all that.

"Get a good nanny," was her hilarious and immediate response. "I had a wonderful Jamaican woman who stayed with me for a long, long time," she told me. "The first time we met, in 1962, I was doing the Mel Brooks musical, *All American,* at the Winter Garden Theater with Ray Bolger. She was referred to me by a friend in the building who had a nanny from Jamaica and asked her nanny if she could recommend somebody. She

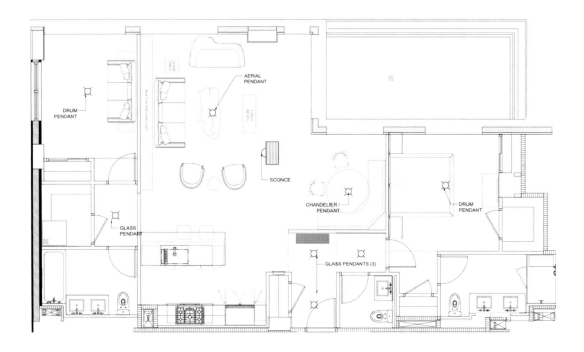

said her friend, Linda, was very good and so we made an appointment for a Saturday morning. She showed up an hour early and I was still in my pajamas which were purple flannel with little yellow elephants on them (because I used to buy clothes in the girls' department!). When I answered the door, she said, 'Is your mother home?' And I said, 'I am the mother.'

And she said, 'Oh, you poor thing.' And she stayed with me for fourteen years! I took her everywhere I went."

Anita's voice and personality can fill the biggest Broadway venues, but she is diminutive in size. I have long referred to her as a "pocket rocket!!"

There is a marvelous New York Times column in the Real Estate section called *The Hunt,* with stories about folks' searches for renting and buying property in New York City. When I was searching to relocate from a one-room studio to a one-bedroom apartment on the Upper West Side, writer Joyce Cohen interviewed me for this feature and titled the piece, *This Neck of the Woods, Please,* because of my rigidity about staying within certain neighborhood parameters. I ultimately acquiesced at the urging of my real estate agent to move a bit out of my comfort zone (the absolute right decision). Joyce has seemingly seen it all when it comes to the trials and tribulations, the highs and the lows, of The Hunt so I wanted to engage her and some of my other most talented brokers with some guidance on how to approach this very important initial phase of working toward manifesting our Dream Home. Also, I want you to meet my award-winning Manhattan real estate broker, Jessica Cohen, my former running-coach-turned-agent Christopher Baker, and Rick Llanos who helped me buy and sell my Los Angeles home. Rick says he's never been busier both buying and selling, since the dawn of Covid-19.

Nelson: Why is it important to work with professionals when hunting for one's Dream Home, rather than doing everything on your own?

Joyce: Unless you know what you're doing—and have done it before— you are bound to make mistakes. Some of these might fall into the sins-of-omission category. There are all sorts of things you won't think about until later—like whether the water pressure really delivers and whether that through-the-wall air conditioner means a cold draft all winter.

Jessica: Different tricks come up in deals that a professional can spot and protect you from. A pro can help keep the process smooth and efficient, saving you time and guesswork. They may also be able to advise you on what trends they are seeing.

Rick: We work for free for the buyer and can usually help them get a better price on a house. Also, depending on the market, there may be homes offered off market that only the realtors know about. There is a lot to do when buying a house, especially during the inspection process. Best to have someone there to help guide you through what's important and when you should walk away.

Christopher: Real estate professionals know other agents, they know the territory, the market, where to look and they work for you, so your satisfaction is their priority.

Nelson: What adjustments did you have to make because of the pandemic?

Jessica: Selling was easier when we could host open houses and meet new buyer prospects and see the flow of traffic that would or wouldn't

attend. Reading a buyer's reaction to a property was easier without a mask! I think technology seemed to be a threat to brokerage before the pandemic as big companies like Zillow suggested that buyers could make deals without a live broker representing them. This period showed people how much we all need human contact, and in some ways assured us we are needed, and buyers aren't as comfortable purchasing without a trusted, live, professional confidant.

Nelson: How should buyers prepare for "the Hunt" to find their Dream Home?

Joyce: Spend a lot of time scrutinizing listings. And going to open houses if possible. That way, you will learn how well

(or badly) the listings correspond to the reality. You will learn the magic of a wide-angle lens, which can make even a cramped bathroom look spacious. And why the curtains are drawn in all the listing photos. And that a photo doesn't show the quality of the finishes or workmanship. Be skeptical of everything.

I went to one open house on a nice spring day. Every window was open and big fans were blowing. A cat hoarder lived in the building, but all the moving air eradicated the smell.

Everyone has different preferences. People may claim they want outdoor space, but they almost never use it, unless they garden or go outside to smoke. Generally, people want natural light. That's easy to check out ahead of time. After the fact, they complain about noise, which is hard to check out. People like high floors for light and views, but that may come with a burdensome wait for a slow elevator.

I suggest that people know what drives them crazy and avoid that, because avoiding what makes you miserable is most important. Of course, some things are fixable and some are not. You can change the hinge on a refrigerator that opens backward. You cannot change the bus stop right outside. Sometimes the most important things about an apartment are outside its four walls.

Jessica: Nobody gets everything, so you will ultimately choose between your wants and needs. Think about how you live and start by listing what you can't live without.

Rick: Get yourself pre-approved to buy and know what you can comfortably afford to spend. Have all your finances in order so when the perfect house comes up, you're ready to go. Also, check out the market, go to open houses so you can see what homes go for and you'll be more aware of values.

Christopher: Yes, get your paperwork done quickly and early so that when it comes time to make an offer, it can happen fast and efficiently. Try and have as much cash liquidity as possible. This will make everything easier in the end.

Nelson: What can make the process easy or fun? (Personally, I find "the Hunt" the most fun part!)

Joyce: That depends on whether someone has time pressure or financial pressure, how much they like their agent, and their general temperament. Some people feel bereft when their hunt is over. Others can't wait until it's over. In general, it is good to live below your means, because you never know when you will encounter a rainy day.

Jessica: Work with a fun broker whom you trust and enjoy. Don't let anyone rush you. A home is a lifestyle. You can try on how the options feel and enjoy the freedom to have choices.

Rick: Don't think there is only one dream house out there for you.

Be open minded. I once had some clients insisting that they only wanted to buy a 1920s Spanish home. A few months later they bought a 1960s ranch house. They had never realized how well it would work for their lifestyle. And don't judge a book by its cover. Even if it looks odd on the outside, it could be in a great area and have a great interior. Don't keep yourself from looking at a place just because it doesn't look like your dream house. Nelson: What if the Dream Home becomes a Nightmare?

Jessica: Don't panic. Explore your options carefully and get advice from the pros around you that you trust. Believe that everything happens for a reason.

Christopher: Don't despair. There are so many different variables that there are bound to be some snags along the way. One more reason to have a seasoned agent on your team.

I asked Christopher about his own experience transforming his wonderful fifth-floor walkup brownstone apartment on the Upper East Side back into a "dream home" after he and his wife divorced, and she moved out (he kept the cat!). Aside from discovering a lot more closet space and room in the medicine chest, he made a single tweak that dramatically altered the vibe of his entire abode.

Christopher: It took me a few months after my divorce to realize I had the ability to make changes. I happened to be in conversation with my friend Brian who was telling me about a vinyl record he had just purchased and listened to. I happen to be really into music, and I explained how jealous I was that he had a turntable setup. Brian responded with, "But Chris, aren't you divorced, and don't you live on your own? You should get a turntable."

"Brian, you're a genius!" I replied. "The next week I had my turntable set up in my living room and was enjoying The Beatles' *Rubber Soul,* with a glass of wine. It was the perfect decision.

Curb appeal isn't just for the suburbs. Besides the outdoor landscaping and building exterior, be sure to thoroughly check out the neighborhood, at various times and days of the week. For me, the proximity of a drug store, dry cleaner and public transportation were as desirable and important as the residential amenities. You can change almost anything about a house . . . except where it's been built!

Interestingly, my friend for four-plus decades, effervescent film and television star Carol Lynley, only ever seemed to be concerned with the outdoor aspects of her residence . . . and not the residence itself. Maybe because she was born in the Bronx, NYC, or perhaps because she was born under the sign Aquarius: she only cared about being near the water! As her acting career wound down in the 1990s, she found the freedom she'd never had to just drift to what made her feel most free: life along the ocean. She opted for modest, low maintenance digs along the Pacific Ocean . . . from Santa Monica to Malibu and finally to Pacific Palisades. She was happiest with no frills inside, but the surf and sunshine right outside. Her interior

was bare bones: a day bed and a microwave, but outside on her long ocean-facing deck were scores of lovingly attended pots filled with flowers, vegetables and herbs of every kind (mostly legal). Her homegrown basil was the key ingredient to her delectable pesto sauce.

Is a safe environment a concern for you as well? Crime statistics are readily available through the web page of your local police precinct, and it's also worth stopping in to chat with the commanding officer or other members of the force. They are neighbors, too, and establishing a friendly, courteous dialogue early on can go a long way in reassuring your sense of security. I have them on speed dial and it's not uncommon for me to drop off a box of cookies or doughnuts if I'm walking by the station. Now, more than ever, they appreciate the support of the citizenry they serve.

Creating your dream home doesn't necessarily mean you're worried about its resale value. If you're like me, it's always in the back of your mind. Real estate is a major investment and can almost always be a profitable one. But you can't let an uncertain market future deter you from recognizing today's joys. Sure, cultivating our extensive outdoor opportunities will help with the apartment's ultimate resale, but a three-bedroom turned into a one-bedroom might repel most prospective buyers, though it was the absolute right decision for us. Restoration Hardware fixtures are always crowd pleasers, but do they reflect your individuality? Remember: your dream home is for you. As spectacular as Oz's Emerald City was, Dorothy learned the hard way that "there's no place like home," even if it's a simple Kansas farmhouse. If you're primarily interested in selling "up," that's a different book altogether.

Don't discount the positive power of Karma. Sometimes a good "feeling" or "vibe" about a place is an excellent indicator of its potential. When I was looking for my Upper West Side one-bedroom co-operative apartment, I purchased it from a young couple who were madly in love with it but had outgrown the space. They went on to have twins soon afterwards and stayed right in the immediate neighborhood, only a block away. They became good friends based on our shared love of Apartment 3A. Then, when it was time for me to sell, I received three offers and went with the one from the buyer with the most personal passion for it. She and I have consequently become friends and I recently introduced her to the original owners and now there are three "generations" of homeowners who all experienced the identical mojo of that lovely, sunny spot. I have a sense that the tradition will continue.

When your hunt is finally over and you've mailed off your Change of Address card, try to remind yourself that dreams change as we go through the stages of life . . . and there may very well be another search in your future. For us, it will be wherever we settle for our retirement and decide to turn that into another adventure: exploring possible locations across the country, for now as holidays, until that time comes. *Search for Tomorrow* isn't just the name of a great old soap opera: it's an optimistic way of living!

Setting the Stage

_____

How do two people (no matter how happily domesticated) with very different tastes and two lifetimes of beloved belongings, merge their possessions into one, uncluttered collection? In my experience, it requires a whole lot of Compromise and a whole lot of Letting Go. When I sold my three-bedroom house in Los Angeles to relocate to a tiny little one-room apartment in Manhattan, I had amassed a lifetime of not only household wares and furnishings, but generations of family heirlooms and collectibles. Everything from my grandparents' wedding china to Cousin Mary's player piano, Mom's silver collection and my own massive stashes of comic book and silver screen mementoes. I sold what I could (thank you ebay), gifted treasures to friends and relatives and donated the rest. I learned to become ruthless in the Purge!

"Never love something that can't love you back" became my mantra . . . and it's the best advice I can give to anyone facing separation anxiety from a library of books or closet full of clothes (the if-you-haven't-worn-it-in-a-year-get-rid-of-it rule is a wise one). As I recently helped my mother prepare to depart her house of thirty-five years for a more minimal lifestyle in an assisted living facility, I was again reminded to practice what I preach!

Wedding the lives of two people to create a beautiful home requires a plan. And, in most cases—certainly in ours—a professional to help. Be objective about knowing your limitations and what you can or cannot do for yourself. I bet you've made more than a few mistakes you can learn from! It's up to an individual to determine how/when they want to economize, but there was no doubt we needed an interior designer to help us sort through it and fine-tune everything to create a plan that would bring us not only the aesthetics we desired, but all the pleasure and convenience we craved. Jonny had successfully worked with a talented designer on his home, but the fellow had moved out of state. We wanted someone who could be always on site and hands-on, and someone who could be truly objective. After interviewing several referrals, we met with Rebecca Roberts, founder and principal of Method & Moxie, a full-service interior architecture and design firm. As so often is the case, timing is everything. Rebecca was the right person at the right time, and she quickly became the third member of our Domestic Partnership!

Since our penthouse (and the rest of the entire 71-unit building) was still in its infancy of creation, we were able to work with developer Rony Nortman and his talented team of contractors and subcontractors from early on—an immense advantage for placement of everything from electrical outlets to the walls, themselves. If you need to hire a contractor, don't skimp on getting referrals and then backing it up with plenty of research. The very "bones" of your home are in their hands!

Working with our developer gave us options: Lemay & Escobar tiles, white oak flooring, Cesar cabinetry, Calcutta quartz countertops and Kohler black matte fixtures. Even with the beautiful architectural features of an Isaac & Stern building, it would be a titanic undertaking. Fortunately, in addition to high-end appliances and all the electronic bells-and-whistles built into the property, Rebecca and Rony collaborated easily to navigate the complicated technical aspects involved with brand-new construction.

We were vigilant about the not-so glamorous but vital aspects of getting all the requisite insurance and documentation for all the tasks ahead. Getting in on the ground floor (no pun intended) was a great help and being able to continue working with the very artisans and experts behind the overall project was a gift. They had a vested interest and desire in making sure we (and all the first residents of the building) were happy. If things are done correctly from the beginning, they will stand the test of time. Finding craftsmen who take pride in their work almost always results in quality. One day, we bumped into a carpenter who was working on another floor of the building, and we struck up a conversation about the job he was doing.

He beamed when he patted the wall and told us, "When I walk by, I say this is my building." Assembling your workforce, regardless of how large or small the job, should feel like a team effort.

A note about Contractors and Designers: Once you have engaged the services of these professionals and mutually set out the parameters of their duties—and your expectations—try not to micromanage. Having a regular dialogue to keep the communication is important, but don't nag about every little item on the To-Do/Punch Lists. For us, Monday mornings were a great time to look at what was planned for the week ahead, then check in on Fridays to see exactly what was accomplished. I also liked to drop in at the job site at unexpected times to see for myself who was there and what they were working on. It's also a good way to make sure things are being executed in safe, orderly, efficient ways.

Aesthetically, we needed to determine the overall look that would reflect us. Your home should tell your story. It is literally the stage upon which your story plays out. Rebecca's training in Interior Architecture and Design from Parsons would help her devise custom installations and unique design elements based on our most important pieces of art.

While my partner and I may have vastly different tastes in that area, we both have great ardor for Modern Art in general. One of our first dates was to the astounding Barnes Foundation in Philadelphia and we have spent the years since traveling the world's most revered museums to appreciate, study and (sometimes) collect. From the Rodin Museum in Paris and the Tate in London to obscure little galleries in South Africa and Australia, art "tourism" is as much a part of our holidays as the hotels and restaurants we visit. Mid-20th Century Modernism was our common denominator, so it was there that Rebecca would begin to draw her inspiration to define the space, materials and color palette. Exercise caution with trends. You want to find classic elements in anything you choose and adjust as refreshes become needed.

Hugh Jackman and his designer wife Deborra-lee Furness spent six years planning and building their East Hampton home which *Architectural Digest* described as an "airy, minimalist dream." Deb says her love of travels to Aman resorts contributed to her desire for such an expansive, monochromatic style ("I can't do primary colors," she insists) but she cleverly plopped a gorgeous open kitchen right into the middle of things to

give it a personal touch. After all, fancy vacation pads are great to visit, but I wouldn't want to live in one! I know some people do. In fact, I know one fellow out in the Hamptons who dropped a ridiculous bundle of dough to achieve his dream of making the entire first floor of their house "look just like a hotel lobby!" Call the bellhop.

My partner came into our union with some impressive, sculptured pieces and several large oil paintings by Theo Tobiasse (1927-2012), a Palestinian born French Expressionist. I had three paintings by William Weintraub (1926-2017), an American born Israeli best known for portraiture. Interestingly, both men shared many biographical similarities if not professional ones. Jonny became aware of Tobiasse while studying in Paris, while the Weintraubs were a lifelong part of my family home, my parents having acquired them when forced to flee a Middle Eastern holiday tour that included Jerusalem when the Six Day War broke out in 1967. Along with two small oils from Northern Italy I had purchased from the same time period and a beautiful serpentine interpretation of Niobe (in Greek mythology the personification of maternal sorrow!) my talented mother chiseled many years ago, these pieces all seemed to complement each other in style, color and form. These were the nuclei for Rebecca and every bespoke item, wall covering, fabric and lighting fixture she would source for our consideration.

For one of the Weintraubs, Rebecca and I had great fun witnessing her expert framer arrange for its restoration, after more than a half-century of

exposure had left it cracked, dingy and faded. Then we found sleek new frames for them both that refreshed them for their new lives in New York City. Isn't it fun to trace the histories of objets d'art as they pass hands and move around through time and space? If you're like me, you keep track of as much history as possible about any given item and record it for posterity.

We also treated lighting as art, not only for the lumens lighting provides functionally, but as actual art pieces. A lot of our budget went into our designer working with artisans to create custom pieces to our specs. For example, a simple nub of glass became a stunning fourteen-inch globe pendant for our office in hues of orange and grey to match the rest of the room. As Rebecca notes, "Glass is a fascinating material to work with and introducing bands of color complicates the process. How and where the colors will expand and how they will interact and change as the glass is blown is a little bit of mystery and part of the beauty of the end product. For us, the light fixtures are every bit as valuable as the paintings on the walls.

What is (or what do you want to be) the focal point of each room of your home? Everything should be designed around drawing the eye to that, whether it's a piece of art, a dramatic view, a big-screen TV or fireplace. "Purposeful Design" means form and function, smart and stylish. Take advantage of any preexisting asset whether it's a majestic tree outside the window or beautiful moulding work in the architecture. Use lighting to highlight and enhance these; even though we love brightness, all our lights are on dimmers so that we can control the mood as needed. Area rugs are another way to create and delineate space, especially with popular open floor plans. Something as simple and seemingly unnoticed as a door trim, crown molding or baseboards can dramatically enhance a room.

I am a big fan of having LIFE all throughout the home. And I don't mean some eye-popping sofa bolsters or wild, overhead mobile . . . I am referring to something that actually has/had a living state. A potted plant, a vase of flowers (fresh cut or artfully dried) or even a bowl of fruit. A tropical fish tank is expensive and inconvenient to maintain unless you have a passion for it, but a decorative glass bowl with a pretty goldfish swimming around is cheap and cheerful — and easy to replace as needed. Since I wasn't blessed with a green thumb, we have low maintenance plants in our bathrooms: a cactus and a "ZZ" (Zamioculcas). On the kitchen counter is a stunning moss bowl.

On a particularly memorable holiday to Vietnam, I couldn't resist bringing home some pretty seashells from "our" beach, which are now in a little porcelain bowl on the bathtub. It suggests outdoor life and brings happy memories every time I glance at it.

Not everyone will have the same taste as we do. It would be boring if everyone liked the same thing! You have to hone in on what your "signature" is . . . what feels right and best expresses YOU. Carefully scrutinize your treasures and then start paring down. Whoever said "less is more" was right when it comes to your decor. Your dream home is also your sanctuary . . . your nest. It isn't Buckingham Palace or Graceland! One good thing that came out of Covid lockdowns was how many folks rediscovered the satisfaction of cleaning out and reorganizing their closets. A good habit to keep up beyond just Spring Cleaning.

Thank goodness for storage so you have a place for things that don't fit in with your new digs, but with which you still can't bear to part. In 1987, when I was a young actor, I was working on the daytime drama, *One Life to Live,* and its scenic designer, the late Macdonald Eaton (1930-2013) was a respected painter in addition to his day job on the set of the soap. He was a sought-after talent in the early days of TV entertainment, working with everyone from Fosse & Verdon, Dick Clark, Victor Borge and Ed Sullivan to Sammy Davis Jr, Kate Smith and Helen Hayes! He painted huge portraits of several members of the cast and crew, myself included, for an exhibit in the studio lobby. It was a great honor for me as a youngster, to be hanging alongside so many TV veterans. After the event, he gifted the painting to me, and it hung in my parents' home for decades after—a very "Eighties" piece of memorabilia that certainly had a *Picture of Dorian Gray* aspect to it. When my widowed mother moved into Assisted Living in 2021, the portrait finally had to come down from the wall and, although I'm sure Eaton's works command a respectable price, who else would want it? Storage was the right answer and there it remains until we can figure out an appropriate way to part with it. Any takers? If nothing else, it's a fun reminder of a bygone era, with my mullet hairdo and past penchant for turtlenecks, ha!

I admit that Jonny and I both tend toward obsessive compulsive cleanliness and order. "Everything in its place" can be impossible to achieve when you're in the middle of a construction, renovation or design project.

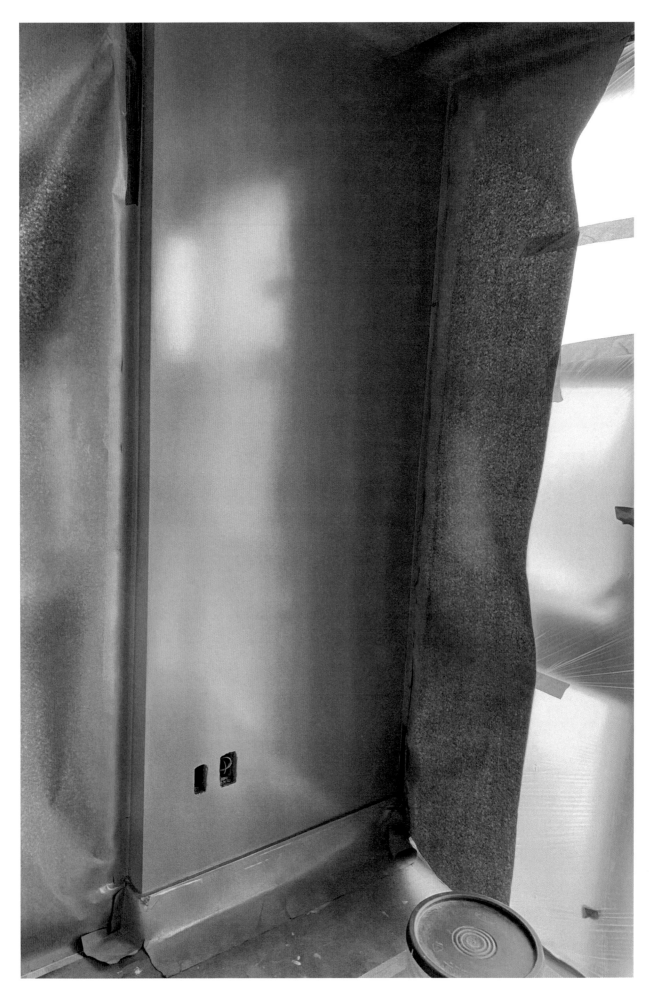

If possible, try to embrace the mess! Someone told me to "Praise the process," which I thought was clever. As a marathon runner, it is sweet to cross the finish line, but the 26.2 miles I have to run to get there also bring me pleasure and satisfaction. One way to help me cope with the (temporary) disorder was to take a lot of pictures of the evolution so I could eventually compare the "before" to the beautiful, finished product and appreciate how far we'd come. We engaged our housekeeper to periodically come in and do as much damage control as she could, and we also treated ourselves to a professional service to do a deep, thorough cleaning before the final move-in. Many features in our home can't be cleaned with paper towels and some Windex or Endust, so careful housekeeping is a must. When treating yourself to custom pieces, be sure to inquire about their ongoing care.

Everyone's idea of the perfect place to live is different. As the youngest of five kids, I can testify that none of us shares a remotely similar lifestyle. A Manhattan apartment in the middle of bustling Harlem would be anathema to my sister, whose idea of heaven is her fishing boat in the Florida Keys . . . or my brother in the Pennsylvania suburbs with lots of farmlands and open skies. To each his own. Even my best friend of forty years, and the most diehard Manhattanite I know, was all but driven out of the city between the pandemic and his job relocating to neighboring Connecticut. It was off to Long Island for him. For outdoorsy, water-loving Australians, Covid-19 resulted in unprecedented growth in the home swimming pool industry.

No matter where you make your home, it can be your castle. It's as much a sensibility as it is a design execution. One of the smartest, most lovely people I know is broadcast journalist and television personality Meredith Vieira. When I told her I was working on this book, I asked her if she had a tip to share, as she seems to have struck the ideal balance between city and country living. When it comes to creating her perfect nest, she admitted, "I certainly have attempted to do that several times. Usually, I start by sitting silently in the space and eventually it reveals itself. For me, everything revolves around the home's place in nature. I see everything organically, probably because I am an earth sign. So, all our homes through the years have relied on outside influences to define the vibe . . . tons of light and greenery. Water and critters always welcome . . . bees, butterflies, birds, bunnies. Although outdoors please," she added with a laugh. "And I don't think a house is a home without a fireplace and the smell of something delicious baking in the oven. Add in two sleepy cats and a dog and a bed you can literally fall into . . . that's a home."

When the Pandemic hit NYC, some friends departed Manhattan, seemingly for good. One of the most surprising for me was diehard city boy and renowned photographer Ben Watts, brother of the marvelous actress Naomi Watts. He himself possesses movie-star looks and charisma and, when I joined Naomi on the set of a commercial she was shooting and met Ben for the first time, I was instantly captivated by his charm and energy. No wonder big stars like Hugh Jackman, Drew Barrymore and Michelle Williams all seek him out when it's time to be captured by the photographic lens. With an eye also for fashion, active living and hip-hop culture, his work frequently appears in publications like *Elle, Vogue, Vanity Fair, Cosmopolitan* and *Rolling Stone.* Even though he was born in the UK and raised in Australia, I never thought he'd leave for the outer boroughs, but he decided to make his holiday home in Montauk, Long Island, his primary residence and (so far) he hasn't looked back. I think it's a wonderful quality to "never say never" and be open to shaking up your life by changing up your residence.

Nelson: Your NYC digs were pretty sweet, Ben. Wasn't that your dream home? What prompted you to resettle and what elements of the city place did you bring to Long Island?

Ben: The beach, and the love of it, took us out to Montauk. I still love NYC, but there's definitely time to appreciate life in Montauk now. We brought a lot of art because I wanted the place to have an "urban NYC beach vibe."

Nelson: What qualities make up what you'd consider your dream home?

Ben: My dream home would have room for all my family and friends at any given time. Lots of rooms with ensuites. I'm very happy with what I have in Montauk, but if it were bigger, I'd like that, too.

Nelson: Was there any compromise or customization work to be done?

Ben: Not really, but I definitely realized that a weekend home could be designed better when you're using it full time. We have put in a massive outdoor kitchen that we are very excited about. We absolutely want it comfortable for everybody.

Nelson: You've lived in many places. Has your perception of the ideal home changed as time goes on?

Ben: I've lived in Kent in the UK, North Wales on a little island called Angelsea, London, Sydney, NYC and now Montauk. When I lived in Wales, I fell in love with the beach, even in winter . . . so I loved living in Sydney. Montauk is just perfect. The beach energizes you. We take dips in mid-winter and it's amazing! I'm very thankful for our spot of Paradise. And it's driving distance to the world's greatest city!

Nelson: Do you see yourself finally staying put or might there be more moves in the future?

Ben: I see myself getting older in Montauk, for sure. Of course, I'm always thinking about expanding and we have already. We call it, "Montaukdreaming."

Nelson: You've shot celebrities all over the world. Was there any particular home that especially influenced or impressed you?

Ben: Honestly, there have been so many great ones, but I recently got to see Anderson Cooper's place and I gotta say, I loved the art and interior design.

Nelson: Your sister, Naomi, lives nearby with her kids. Do you have similar senses of style?

Ben: In some cases, yes. In others, no. She's more practical and functional than me!

Nelson: I'm always impressed with the dazzling use of color in your photography. How do you use color in your home?

Ben: I did a lot myself but also worked closely with an interior designer named Staci Dover, who also did my sister's place. My home is eccentric and it's pretty obvious when you enter that I live there!

Nelson: Any advice for people who long to achieve their own dream home?

Ben: Never stop dreaming and work extremely hard. That's how I did it. I always dreamt of buying my neighbors' properties on both sides and expanding. And it happened, but not without hard work.

Nelson: Is it true that your home is your castle—and if so, are you the King?

Ben: It is absolutely true. There is no place like home and it's important to create a comfortable, welcoming home that has personality and warmth. You want people to feel good and share fondest memories. Then you have a Kingdom.

For Jonny and me, individuality and variety in design and execution (like any other aspect of life!) is what makes a house a home. Making an "ours" rather than sticking with a "his" or "mine" is what started the journey for me. What will it be for you??

For many years, I've enjoyed the reporting of my colleague, Robert Jobson, the esteemed author and expert on all things royal. In addition to his many books and regular TV reporting on the subject, he was also the consultant on the scripted series, *Royals,* starring Elizabeth Hurley and Dame Joan Collins and even made cameo appearances as himself! Since the theme of this book is make your home feel like your castle, I thought I'd take the opportunity to get his thoughts on how the Windsors and their kind do the same . . . even when they're living in ACTUAL castles! As always, he never disappoints with his insight into their particularly posh world!

Nelson: They say, "a man's home is his castle," but when it comes to the Royals, what makes their castle(s) a home?

Robert: Members of the royal family have several properties around the UK, and in Prince Charles's case two properties in Romania. They each have their own style, their own interior designers and decorators, and make sure that they are kitted out exactly how they wish — paid for by their own private money, and in some cases on structural repairs, public money.

Nelson: Like every family, each of the Windsors is an individual. Is there a common thread that they all have when it comes to their homes? (Besides a security detail!).

Robert: The most important thing for the Windsor family when it comes to their homes is privacy. When the queen gave William and Kate Amner

Hall, they spent a small fortune on having new trees and mature hedging planted to prevent the paparazzi taking photographs of them from a distance. It is important for them that when their children are out playing in the garden, they cannot be snapped by long lens photographers. A lot of the current properties that are established royal properties already have that sort of security built in, because in the Windsor Castle there are high castle walls.

Nelson: Can you name any certain things that really make a cold, drafty palace seem like a "home" to them?

Robert: The properties of the royal family are not particularly cold and drafty, except for Balmoral. Birkhall, Charles's Scottish home, is cozy. He spends a lot of time there in his study. On the walls outside, beautiful prints have characters from Victorian England packed on the corridor walls. There are fires and central heating . . . they do have the modern conveniences that most modern homes would have. Buckingham Palace is currently a building site; nobody is living there. There are 775 rooms in the palace, including 52 royal and guest bedrooms, 188 staff bedrooms and 92 offices. There are also 78 bathrooms in the building.

Nelson: Who are the interior designers for the Royals?

Robert: The queen spends an awful lot of time at Windsor Castle, in her private apartments where her rooms are very much of her time.

They even have old radios, old televisions, in the rooms. Any other changes to the queen's residence are handled by the Keeper of the Privy Purse—her accountant—who puts the work out to tender. They don't really like to change their style. If you look at Prince Charles's property in Dumfries House in Scotland, it's beautifully designed by professional interior designers and contains priceless antique furniture, much of it by Chippendale. Dudley Poplack was Diana's interior designer who carried out work at Apartments 8 and 0 and Kensington Palace. Charles often uses his sister-in-law, Annabel Elliot (Camilla's sister) to carry out interior design work for his properties. William and Kate used one of Charles's finds to help with their country home, Anmer Hall, and their apartment 1A at Kensington Palace. The man who knows the palace's design secrets is the 49-year-old architectural designer Ben Pentreath, who has been on speed dial with the royal family since 2009, when Prince Charles first enlisted his services, and who has become especially well known for his work for Prince William and Kate Middleton on Amner Hall.

Nelson: What would surprise us to find in a Royal home?

Robert: You wouldn't necessarily think of them as regal.

Nelson: What's something in the queen's residence that the average person could emulate or aspire to having in their own?

Robert: The Queen surrounds herself with historical objects, trinkets and personal mementos that she keeps close at hand. She has certain cushions placed on a wooden dining chair for extra height and comfort and uses a modern Apple computer when she's speaking to foreign dignitaries on

Zoom or over the internet. She has a simple wooden desk with two small drawers and assorted royal photos. There is one by (Annie) Leibovitz, which she particularly likes. She has things like a very ornate wall mirror, heavy gold curtains, and a settee with floral upholstery. She uses an old telephone, which is white, and quite sweet really! She also has a little statuette of a queen's guard on the top right of her desk and an antique cabbage leaf plate, and bowl.

Little things make it homey. Her love of corgis is well documented, and she has little figurines of them in silver. There's also one in china, and two smaller ones, thought to be silver on a slate block. She has three horse statuettes in the center. There's a miniature rider on horseback, possibly meant to be a model of the queen herself.

Nelson: I would imagine it's a challenge for a royal to be a minimalist!

Robert: The royals are surrounded by books and book cabinets. Particularly Prince Charles; he's quite cluttered. He also surrounds himself with family photographs at Birkhall and Clarence House and Highgrove. He is always surrounded by piles of books and photographs and has hand-painted watercolors, too. His books range from philosophy books to novels by thriller writer and ex-jockey Dick Francis left over from the queen mother. He too has lots of framed photographs of his family around. There is one that Charles loves on display: with him, the queen, Prince Phillip and the queen mother together at a black-tie function. He also has a photograph of his grandson, Archie, with a miniature stuffed teddy bear with a bow tie.

Nelson: What is the most "homey" of the royal residences?

Robert: They're all individual in style, but I would say probably the homiest residence would be Birkhall because it's where the queen mother lived. Prince Charles would have added his personality to it as well but kept many of the features. It is a homey residence, smaller than one would think . . . with the lovely, lawn that sweeps down to the river, which the prince can see from his study.

While the Windsors may have literal castles for their homes, the rest of us must make do with what is within our reach. A large space is wonderful if you have the content and lifestyle to fill it. Sometimes, a compact and efficient abode works out for the best. My elderly mother learned that when we finally convinced her to downsize from the rambling, museum-like house she and my father had occupied for nearly four decades to a smart and sunny apartment. Not only did she make a tidy profit on the sale of the property, but she discovered the fun and ease of apartment living . . . something she'd never tried in over nine decades of life.

My lifelong friend, Alexandra Boyd, is not only an accomplished actor and filmmaker, she is also a cunning designer and has parlayed those skills into being a successful AirBnB host, specializing in converting small properties into fabulous, functional living spaces. I've seen her do it with Hobbit-sized cottages, guest houses and even a retro Airstream trailer. She's the perfect person to ask for advice on working in cramped quarters.

Nelson: As a designer specializing in "tiny homes," how can you help someone achieve their dream home and still have as many of the design elements a client would want?

Alexandra: In a small space the key is to work with one simple theme. Keep colors and materials to a minimum. White and neutrals all the way through or one or two choices of wood in a similar tone and texture with just a splash of one color. Examples: Modern, light, bright, white, sleek and minimal; cozy, woodsy cabin; industrial container with metal surfaces and repurposed functional furniture.

Nelson: It's hard for people to part with beloved treasures or forfeit amenities. How do you convince them to scale down for a tiny home—and do you have any suggestions to help make this possible?

Alexandra: Yes, it is hard to persuade people to part with heirlooms and treasures but then they must ask themselves why they want to live in a tiny house in the first place? Is it the lower utility costs and the appeal of a mortgage free life? Is it to escape the city and have more outdoor living space? Either way, something has to go! Choose one or two small precious things. You don't have to throw everything out. But be mindful of the need for multi-use of the space and how grandma's dresser just might not function there. A friend of mine recently sold everything she'd accumulated over the last thirty-plus years. She kept only a few essential beloved items. Gone was a basement full of clothes on racks, furniture,

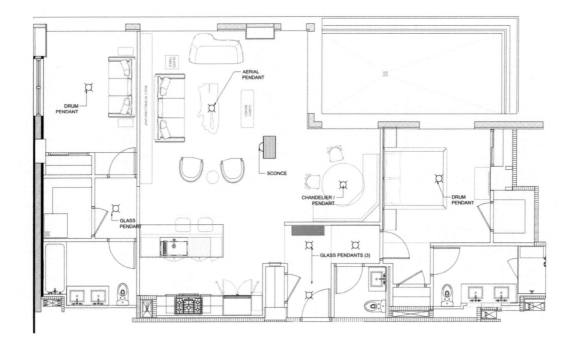

beds, kitchen things. She treated the downsizing as a new beginning and enjoyed the prospect of buying only the essentials for her new compact living space.

Nelson: Where do you begin? I imagine it can be overwhelming. And once it's finished, how do you keep people from eventually bursting at the seams?

Alexandra: The biggest challenge is making the best use of the space and not wasting an inch. Using spaces for more than one purpose, such as a larger sleeping loft, can have the space for a seated workspace. A reading loft can double as a child's sleeping bunk. If you've decided to downsize and have less stuff, you won't need as much closet space. Putting drawers and doors under the stairs to the loft and utilizing cute, space-saving baskets and boxes as part of the decor helps too.

Nelson: Does living in a tiny space necessarily mean you're downsizing?

Alexandra: Yes. It does. There's no room for a grand piano—or even an upright! Most tiny houses only have a shower, foregoing a bathtub. Sometimes it's necessary to shorten the depth of a countertop to make use of a galley kitchen. But it's nice to not have very far to go to the fridge from the sofa to top up your glass of wine (laughs).

Nelson: For some homeowners, a sprawling property is a sign they've made it. What are the perks/advantages of tiny home dwelling?

Alexandra: I don't understand huge houses. Most people don't make the most of all the rooms they have in those huge dwellings. In a tiny house you use every inch, and you know where everything is without searching for hours. If you are organized and good at putting things away in their right place, you can live a small, neat, uncluttered life. Why not spend that money you've made and buy a beautiful property that gives you more space outdoors?

Nelson: Can physically larger individuals be happy in a tiny home?

Alexandra: My boyfriend and I could not live together in a tiny house. Fact. He's six-feet-two, and we are both big personalities to boot. He'd hate hitting his head on the roof of the sleeping loft all the time. But if I were single again, I would love to live in one of the small living spaces I've created. They are perfect for singles, as granny flats or guest houses or, like the one in our forest in Millie's Gulch in Port Ludlow Washington, a delightful AirBnB for short weekend escapes from the city.

Our designer, Rebecca Roberts, has thoughts on the interior design principals you should consider when beginning your project:

True design has a purpose, which differentiates it from art or even décor. Design is thoughtful, considered and with attention to detail. Designers understand those details and define solutions accordingly. Without necessarily being able to identify why, people know when they are in a well-designed space. There are some basic principles of design that are good to keep in mind:

Function — The first thing to consider in a space is how you need it to function. Is it a work/live space? A family friendly space? An intimate, quiet space? An entertaining space? Once you have identified its function you can start to define the elements you need to fulfill that function.

Proportion/Scale — measure your space (including ceiling height) and any furnishings you want to purchase. Long before I learned any software programs to assist in space planning, I used graph paper to scale a room and furnishings. I played with layouts to make sure my furniture would fit in my space. Oversized furniture presents proportional and logistical problems, and undersized pieces get lost and look out of place.

Balance—the concept that from a central point the room appears balanced on either side. That doesn't mean that everything needs to be perfectly symmetrical, but that the visual weight is proportional on both sides of that central point. Distribute your furnishings, artwork, and perhaps draperies to establish this balanced feeling. It doesn't have to be crowded to have balance. Err on the side of giving your furnishings room to breathe.

Interest—visual interest can be achieved through layering textures (hard/soft, smooth/rough), patterns (my preference here is subtle, and playing with the scale of patterns), bringing in color and having some contrast (dark/light). Every room should have a focal point—it might be a special piece of art or a chandelier or sofa that catches your attention first. Be careful not to overdo it—if everything is special, nothing is.

Lighting—often overlooked, this is one of the more critical elements in a room. Consider where you will need different types of lighting for different activities.

Moxie—I can't leave this one out! People ask why my firm is called Method + Moxie, and it is because these are two primary elements in designing any project. Clearly there is a method we follow to ensure we are meeting the needs of the client and the requirements of the space. The moxie is the essential spark that is unique to each client. It drives the inspiration for the entire project. It's your space, so personalize it. A great way to do this is through accents, artwork, photos, preferred pillows or throws, family pieces or great travel finds.

Shop Smart

Setting up a budget is important before starting any new endeavor, especially something as colossal as home design, improvement, creation, or renovation. Even a job you think might be easy and low impact, such as redecorating a kids' room or turning a spare bedroom into a home office, could have all sorts of unexpected costs. It's no fun having to cut corners, but if you prioritize and organize, you'll probably find the most important aspects will all get accomplished, and the extravagances will eventually follow. And what kind of dream keeps you awake at night worrying about bill collectors!?

A "dream home" is different for every person/couple/family, so it isn't possible (or fair) to try and compare costs and expectations with anyone else. Don't give in to the old "Keeping up with the Joneses" mentality or competing with a sibling, old classmate, or colleague. Be yourself, let your home express you and only worry about how it functions and what it means to its inhabitants. If you're moving into a new place, be sure to have an experienced inspector go over everything from top to bottom. It will almost certainly alert you to potential issues that will ultimately save you time and anxiety later.

Did you ever watch reruns of the classic 1960s sitcom, *Green Acres*? Husband Oliver Douglas' idea of the dream home was a ramshackle old farmhouse out in the countryside, while wife Lisa preferred the big city of New York and famously sang in the theme song, "I just adore a penthouse view! Dahhling, I love you but give me Park Avenue!" The man won out and they moved to a life filled with pig sties and hay bales . . . but it became their castle! A decade later, on *The Jeffersons,* George and Louise had a different way of measuring their happiness and success by "movin' on up to a dee-luxe apartment in the sky." They even hired their first housekeeper! Different dreams for different households.

Inspiration boards are useful tools for everyone involved in the project, mixing and matching your ideas and aspirations all along the way. Have you seen any of the design game apps on your Smartphone? They're fun ways to experiment with, and test your skills, too.

I subscribe to several different home and entertainment themed magazines and enjoy tearing out various pages, articles, clippings and other tidbits, and they all go into a file for me to sort through whenever I'm tackling a new project. Obviously, something crafty and homespun from *Better Homes and Gardens* or *Martha Stewart Living* will be different from *Architectural Digest* or *Wine Spectator,* but there's no telling where you might harvest the next great brainstorm! If you're single, you have the freedom to experiment and be more spontaneous, but I find sharing the responsibility with a partner even more satisfying. And, yes, I know I

could be reading all those online, but I do enjoy keeping a "To Read" stack of magazines handy. My TV job requires a lot of waiting around and thumbing through them is a fun distraction.

Much to my partner's embarrassment, I am also a notorious haggler, discount doyenne and coupon clipper! I have a folder stuffed with hundreds of Bed Bath & Beyond coupons. I keep them on hand for whenever I need or want a new set of sheets, towels, coffee maker or pricey beauty product—and I never scoff at comparison shopping. Turning fifty, and then fifty-five (and presumably sixty soon) opens up new worlds of discounts at grocery stores, car rentals, movie theaters and health clubs, and I take full advantage of them whenever possible! So should you. Paying full price should be reserved for items you only desperately require or desire, in my opinion. I must inherit the thrift gene from my dad whose motto was, "No Debt, No Regret." His love of bargaining over sale items would so frustrate my mother that she would often bark, "Be rich!" before insisting on paying full price. I think of him every Tuesday when I find myself at the supermarket's Senior Discount Day. Dad and I never met a generic brand we didn't like!

Thoughtful prioritizing can help you save money and tick items off your Wish List. Outfitting a new home almost entirely from scratch is daunting in every way . . . especially monetarily. A custom Poliform wall unit with individual LED lighting, we decided, was worth the investment (and turned out more sexy, gorgeous and functional than I ever dared imagine) while electronic Crestron® blinds and lighting control was not. We get more use out of the microwave and wine fridge than the other high-end appliances that came with the condo, so that was where our kitchen budget went rather than into any other fancy appliances or accoutrements. That said, quality merchandise pays off . . . and so do manufacturer warranties; be sure to activate them. The advent of Smart TVs was great for us because we aren't binge watchers, unless it's news, and we can also enjoy our music that way, too. Fortunately, most of the equipment in the office is either supplied by my employer or tax deductible, so the funds allocated for that room went to the millwork for an L-shaped, glass-topped desk where we can both work comfortably. Try making a Wish List of everything you're aiming for and/or need most . . . and then write your budget in a column alongside that list. It will become clear immediately where you should be spending dollars first.

If you can't afford to have everything all at once (who can?), we find tremendous reward in contributing to our joint bank account whenever possible . . . knowing that we are working toward the next thing on that List! (You don't need to be a high roller to have a relationship with an advisor at your local bank. They are really very helpful allies in putting together investment plans, as long as you don't get stuck with a "salesman" who wants to lure you into taking out expensive loans.)

The Poliform, an extravagant purchase, was disappointingly assembled when the big day finally arrived after many delays. There were three different "loose ends" I noticed and duly photographed for them to come back and rectify. Sometimes it takes vigilance and persistence if you want to get what you pay for, and for big purchases like that, don't settle for anything less than perfect. On a similar note, it's not a bad idea to save a few outstanding items on your To-Do/Punch List, to keep your contractors or designers engaged and on their toes. I find that we get better-than-average customer service when we behave like better-than-average customers and remain as polite and patient as possible.

Dream big but act smart. Don't live beyond your means—splurge only when/if you can and recognize that, no matter what your budget is, overages and surprise costs are bound to occur. Did you remember to include permits, insurance and materials in your calculations? What about security? What level of protection suits your needs? Again, this is where a professional consultation can be invaluable. Someone who can scrutinize your individual requirements with your living situation and help you formulate a plan that is best for you. Just don't let them "up-sell" you, because I can almost guarantee you, they will try!

There are endless resources and guides to help you get started. From Pinterest to all those DIY TV shows and crafty craftsmen, it can be easy to be fooled into thinking you're only a mouse click away from being able

to whip up your perfect home. But just as you should have a real estate professional assist you with securing a new home, so should you budget and plan for professional assistance when it comes to design. Most of the home furnishings chain stores like Pottery Barn or West Elm will offer consulting services, but keep in mind that the end result will most likely look exactly like the showroom of a Pottery Barn or West Elm, which is fine if that's really what reflects you. I'm betting it isn't.

You may be handy, but that doesn't mean you can expect to do everything yourself. A friend turned us on to taskrabbit.com after we were impressed with the staff she had assembled for a brunch party. You can find an affordable helper for almost any job, from babysitting and copy writing to furniture assembly/disassembly and hanging/connecting TVs and appliances. It's perfect for locating someone in your own neighborhood if you need an extra set of hands or are (like us) all thumbs. Now if I could only find someone to help me learn how to be good on the grill!

One thing I'd never tackle again is self-moving. Well into my fifties, I was still opting to pack up boxes and load them into a U-Haul or friend's SUV. After a certain age, it just isn't worth whatever you think you're saving. That said, a good mover you can trust is hard to find and we've all learned the hard way not to put your blind trust into Yelp reviews or local advertisements. This is one area where you need a referral from someone you can count on. We made a list of all our friends we could think of who have moved often and had major valuable items, then asked them to recommend a company they loved. We got a mere two responses. Turns out, it's harder for a mover to find love than a dentist! Whoever you hire, do your due diligence and make sure that, in addition to an estimate, you properly verify their insurance status and reputation. In this area, try not to leave anything to chance.

Depending on your personality, some purchases are more fun than others. Maybe your idea of a good time is picking out window treatments, throw pillows or bathmats, but even if you're not creating your home from scratch like we did, try to think from the bottom up. How are your fuses?

Do you need leak detectors? What kind of security should you choose for your residence? Make a list, check it twice, and add to it as needed. The "fun stuff" will eventually come.

Delays come with the territory. In our case, Covid brought construction to a grinding halt for several months and, even once we finally got back into the groove, the subsequent slowdowns in every imaginable supply chain—from building materials to linens and switch plates—became a daily occurrence. The world felt the ripple effects in speed and costs. We were fortunate to have the luxury of time and no hard deadlines breathing down our necks, but (especially for punctuality junkies like myself) those inevitable and often unforeseen bottlenecks can be maddening. Try to remind yourself that not only do "good things come to those who wait," but those periods can also give you the opportunity to sleep on things, weigh other options, haggle for discounts and extras or catch up on other items from your Pending List. Chances are, there are zillions . . . and you don't need Siri to help you recalculate when things go awry. No lie: the elevator in our old place died just prior to our firmly scheduled move-out and we were forced to adapt (and pay for) the unexpected change from Easy Access to a four-story-stairwell-walkup. Maddening, but beyond our control.

Customer service, too (alas!), isn't what it used to be. Post pandemic, the workforce hasn't (yet) bounced back to its former level of attention and satisfaction seeking. No one can seem to adequately explain why, but there you have it. I used to beam with pride when foreign friends would gush

over the extraordinary service they enjoyed everywhere in America, from coffee shops to cab rides, but that isn't so much the case as of this writing. When I do encounter exceptional service, however, I am quick to acknowledge and reward it, whether that is in the form of a generous gratuity, a positive review, a glowing email to management or extra/repeat business.

Whenever possible, I encourage engaging local vendors, merchants and craftsmen. Sure, it often seems easier to be a click away from transactions, but in-person interactions can often result in better prices and more dedicated, reliable (and accountable) customer service. Rather than source an outside electrician, maybe you're better off with the one your contractor relies on and trusts. Our building's exterior landscaping service so impressed us that we ended up using them for our own terrace needs, keeping business right in the neighborhood and getting a good discount to boot! I was determined to engage Harlem artistry in our design choices, so Rebecca and I opted to use Sheila Bridge's gorgeous toile in the foyer coat closet. A cunning bit of decor and a nod to our neighborhood.

Rebecca Roberts' Recommendations for Getting Started:

Define a clear scope of work. This is an outline of the project that identifies all work involved. For example, what rooms are you tackling? Does the space function as you need it to or are you changing function? What specific furnishings are you looking to add or replace? What important pieces must stay? Is your lighting sufficient?

Define a budget. Know what you want to spend before you start. It will help you set priorities in terms of the items you want to splurge. It's easy to amortize any spend over the lifetime of enjoyment of that item, but it all adds up.

Is this DIY or are you hiring a designer to help?

Know thyself. Your home is your haven and it should reflect your personality, your history/travels, and your interests.

Find your inspiration. Every project I work on is inspired by something about the client. With one of our projects the client clearly preferred curvilinear lines and shapes, her children had grown up and she wanted to remodel her kitchen. We used a beautiful hand-painted filigree tile for her backsplash and pendant lighting that reflected similar lines, and then carried that theme subtly into other rooms in the form of pillows, drapery details and lighting. A different client had gathered a smattering of furnishings over the years (as we all do) and none of it coordinated. The only thing she and her husband agreed they loved was the colorful and geometric rug, so we discarded everything else and designed the room around the rug.

Be bold and have fun! When I first met Nelson and Jonny they said they wanted to "tear the Band-Aid off" in designing their new penthouse apartment in Harlem. And did we! We curated an interesting mix of wallcovering textures, all warm neutrals, that define individual spaces (living room, dining nook, foyer, bedroom, etc.) while establishing a clear circulation through the space and adding visual interest. We mixed mica, cork, printed silk, silkscreen, mylar and even newsprint, and to contrast so many textures we lacquered specific sections of walls and a ceiling. We had similar fun with textiles on upholstered items, combining wood and glass, and of course with lighting. Pro Tip: When you are making selections, try to get samples of the materials before you make any purchases. The spaces don't have to match, but there should be a flow between spaces (especially in smaller spaces like apartments). With samples in hand, you can organize each room of samples next to each other to ensure they work well together.

Room by Room

Every home is different, but we all have essentially the same basic requirements when it comes to what comprises our abode. Eating, sleeping, washing, working and relaxing. For ease of explanation, I'm breaking this chapter down by the rooms in my particular home. Remember, we started out as a three-bedroom which we converted to one, to enlarge the Great Room to include a dining alcove, and we made the westernmost bedroom into an office. No offense, but even with as much entertaining as we do, we never invite overnight guests. If someone wants or needs to crash, they'll just have to curl up on the sofa with an afghan or pitch a tent on the rooftop! (Or I'm happy to point out the best hotels in the area!)

Speaking of guest rooms, I was struck by an Instagram post by designer Sheila Bridges, often named as one of America's Best Interior Designers and frequently featured on TV and in print for her stylish and practical wisdom (she famously outfitted former President Clinton's 8,300-square-foot Harlem office). She captioned an image of a spare bedroom, "Some nights I like to sleep in my guest room. Just because." I totally understand that! Growing up, visits to my grandmother's house always had an element of surprise because we didn't know which spare room she would assign to us. If you have a lovely extra room that you use in that capacity, consider a "stay-cation" sometime. Sleep around!

Before we get started, this is a good place to address the all-important issue of storage. Whether or not you believe in the powers of feng shui, everyone can agree that a neat and organized abode is not only more visually attractive, but more functionally useful. If you can't bear to part with certain items, or simply don't have enough room for a full four seasons of wardrobe, consider what storage options are available to you — whether that's in your attic/basement/garage or a rented facility. My best friend and his designer partner have a sprawling country house with a basement the size of a bowling alley, so that has not only become a storage facility for them and many of their friends (myself included!) but a de facto warehouse for furniture, rugs, artwork and assorted decor that they can swap out whenever the feel the need for a refresh or re-do. In our apartment building, we have two secure storage cages on a lower floor. One we use for things like luggage, photo albums, a tool kit and a ladder. The other is essentially a closet for off-season clothes, coats and accessories like umbrellas, beach towels, gloves and scarves. Why clog up precious space in the apartment with things you won't be using for another six months? Another great use for accessible storage is to keep framed photos of loved ones and special gifts or mementoes from friends; if these items are convenient to grab, you can make visitors feel special by displaying them in your living space where they can be seen.

Closets are key and customizing them for maximum efficiency was important to us. California Closets® did a top-notch job of customizing our limited ones with ingenious lighted shelving and drawers. Carrie

Bradshaw may have had that huge, walk-in closet and dressing room, but most of us have to make do with much less. Now that we have a sensible system installed (bedroom closets, foyer coat closet, linen closet and office closet to house a printer and various supplies), the challenge for us will be to keep our socks and underwear neat and orderly. Believe it or not, having lighted drawers isn't just helpful for getting dressed in pre-dawn hours without disturbing your partner, it will help ensure you keep them tidy.)

Just as the design and aesthetics should flow seamlessly from room to room throughout your home, so too should the actual air! A clean flow of fresh or filtered air not only keeps the place more temperate, less stuffy but healthier. We were painfully reminded during Covid-19 of how crucial this is. Better breathing for everyone in your family is possible when your dwelling is free of particles and mold, thanks to good air circulation. While you may not be able to control how much outdoor space/access you have, the number of windows or height of the ceilings, you should absolutely take "air" into consideration regardless. Quality windows (especially ones that can help reduce noise and UV damage) are a worthwhile investment, and clean filters for your heating and air conditioning units should be an essential part of your routine home maintenance. Depending on the climate where you live, you may also want to consider adding a dehumidifier/humidifier or air filter to certain areas. Nowadays, there are plenty of quiet and visually unobtrusive models to choose from. Consider attractive fans, especially on higher floors and sunny spots, to aid in proper ventilation and air distribution with the bonus of dissipating odors, fumes and pollutants like dust contaminants and other particulates. Routinely check the sealant around your doors, windows and even fireplaces to help keep control of your air quality. This is especially important if you have family members with breathing issues such as asthma, allergies or COPD.

Your window treatments, too, obviously help with temperature and light control but they also serve to frame/enhance the windows themselves. Make sure they're beautiful, easy to open and close—and clean. Nothing can limit or enhance the spacious feeling of a room like what's surrounding your windows. I learned what a "soffit" is when Rebecca had them built over all our windows to hide the hardware of our shades and draperies, keeping all the rooms sleek looking and maximizing the views.

Our square footage is not massive, in fact it's slightly less than our previous residence but the floor-to-ceiling walls of windows' abundant light and adjacent outdoor space make it look and feel far more spacious. Economizing space was another factor in our design choices . . . another example of opting for quality over quantity!

When you approach our building's entrance, what you see is a modern and serene oasis from the bustling, noisy Harlem streets. The tall, but not too tall, tower of glass and steel reaches to the open sky with an impressive, cantilevered architecture, without distracting from the panoply of the neighboring structures. Locked wooden gates will open to lead you down a long, open entryway with modern lighting and protective glass panels overhead. It is spare, clean and inviting. Alongside the rustic looking wooden fencing are handsome black planters perfectly landscaped by local Harlem florist Franz James. This leads you to the lobby, a tasteful and airy space reminiscent of a boutique hotel, attended by a friendly Concierge. From there, you can take an elevator to the Penthouse floor.

A long, windowed corridor will take you to our apartment and, by then, I assume your shoes will be free of any street debris, but regardless: make sure you are wearing nice socks, because once you ring the doorbell your shoes will have to come off! (Don't fret: if you don't want to leave them in the hallway we have a shoe rack inside the coat closet.)

Come on in and let us give you the tour!

Foyer

They say, "you only get one chance to make a first impression," so we wanted the front door to open into a tidy, welcoming area, free of clutter and with a glimpse of what lies ahead as you move throughout our home. A tall but narrow table inside the doorway is where we drop our keys and masks, but otherwise there is an open space dominated primarily by an enormous Tobiasse lithograph titled, *America,* which shows the artist arriving in New York Harbor. It is modern, dramatic, and thematically ideal to greet visitors. The wall upon which it hangs had originally been part of an additional bedroom we abandoned before it was built, opting for the extra square footage and more unique floorplan. By keeping just one wall, it created not only an extra space for artwork, but a delineation between the foyer and the greater expanse of the main living area.

Underfoot, the handcrafted, custom Lucy Tupo rug made of silk and wool from her native New Zealand, stretches the length of the hallway and perfectly matches the textured wall coverings. Behind the door is a large, circular hanging mirror, and opposite is the coat closet. It is a treat and a clever surprise to open the closet door and see it magnificently lined with Harlem Toile and its whimsical design that blends old patterns with a modern sensibility. We love showing off the closets, so it's good incentive to make sure we keep them neat and orderly. Overhead, three glass pendant lights provide adjustable brightness. They also attract crazy amounts of dust and require constant swiping with a feather duster.

The unavoidable placement of a fuse box accessed behind an ugly metal door is disguised by having had it expertly papered over with the same wall covering, so it's more of a "secret panel".

Powder Room

This not-so-small room tucked right off the foyer is elegant and comfortable for guests who need to "powder their noses." Note: I believe that bathroom doors should never be kept wide open. Leave them slightly ajar to indicate that they're unoccupied should someone wish to use them. To me, a closed bathroom door means someone in there requires privacy.

Small, square black tiles adorn one wall, with small hanging lights and a backlit, round mirror that create a dramatic effect. Black marble floor tiles make it even more handsome, so we decided to really go for it and up the ante by painting the ceiling and walls a stunning charcoal gray lacquer. Growing up, my parents had an all-black powder room and so I found this to be both sophisticated and nostalgic.

The severe, dark tone of the room would be perfect for the two Weintraub paintings I'd had restored/reframed. One depicts a Middle Eastern gentleman looking somberly off into the distance, the only color a tassel of red hanging from his turban and the cerulean blue of his eye. The other is a landscape of an Israeli mountainside with livestock grazing against the dark, tempestuous skies. The overall feeling when you are in there is complete solitude, a stark contrast to the light and almost vivacious atmosphere of the rest of the apartment.

Kitchen

Turning left (west) from the foyer you will enter the Great Room with the kitchen most immediately in sight. As Rebecca taught me, the stunning quartz countertop there is not an island but rather a peninsula, because it actually abuts the wall. The appliances are top notch, with stunning dark Italian cabinetry offsetting the light wooden floors. However, even with the state-of-the-art refrigerator, oven, wine fridge and dishwasher, the developers seemed to omit one very important (and for us, vital) component of the kitchen: a microwave! They must have realized it somewhere along the way, because when the deal for the place was finally secured, a tiny little microwave magically appeared tucked into one of the cabinets. It would barely have sufficed in a dormitory room, so we picked out a large, attractive one to sit atop the counter beside the stove. A brief consideration had been made to install some kind of cabinetry that would house the appliance, but with as much use as we get out of it, it was more important that it be easily accessible. Don't get in my way when I need to heat up a cup of coffee or defrost some lasagna! (A double freezer with ice maker ensures we can always keep ourselves stocked with a massive supply of leftovers, frozen treats and doggy bags from our favorite restaurants.)

That aside, the kitchen design is thoughtful and ample, with a massive pull-out pantry adjacent to the fridge. It is truly a chef's paradise. If only we had a chef!

The counter of the peninsula could easily accommodate four stools, but we opted for three to create more elbow room when enjoying a bar meal (which we love). One of the first things we tested was the available space underneath the countertop so that our knees didn't bump into it when sitting at the bar. You'd be surprised what a common design flaw that is in many kitchens! Rebecca guided us toward some beautiful choices from B&B Italia that not only had lower back support, but swivel seats. Jonny wanted each stool upholstered in a different color fabric, but I persuaded him to go for all three in the same, neutral tone to match the Great Room. We already had enough color variation going on . . . I wanted these to remain simple and unadorned.

There is, however, a playful pop of color on the kitchen wall with a whimsical, large painting of a giant bowl of red cherries. It's simple but bold, and elicits a smile from anyone who knows that "life is just a bowl of cherries!" Franz James fulfilled my desire for a dramatic moss bowl atop the counter, complimenting the artwork perfectly.

While we're still in the kitchen, this is a good time to introduce you to another one of my fab friends, Kate Heddings. She is an author and contributing editor to *Food & Wine,* so she certainly knows her way around this part of the house! She obliged me with some answers I was dying to know!

Nelson: As a food and wine authority, how much time do you spend in your kitchen at home as opposed to out in the field?

Kate: I'm probably cooking in my kitchen four nights a week, and I'm out to dinner three nights. But since I work from home now, I make lunch (as well as breakfast) daily, so I feel like I'm in the kitchen all the time.

Nelson: Is your current kitchen your dream kitchen? If so, what makes it that for you?

Kate: I adore my kitchen. The only thing missing is more space—NYC kitchens are rarely big enough! We renovated a few years back so now it's an open kitchen, with plenty of open counter space, lots of storage (including an ample pantry and large deep kitchen drawers). I also love shiplap and wanted something like that for my backsplash, but not actual shiplap, which would be silly in a modern NYC apartment. (Note: Shiplap is a wooden board most often used as an exterior siding for barns and sheds.) So we found beautiful long white stone slabs and my backsplash is exactly right. We did pretty, high gloss white cabinets and they reflect such nice light back into the whole open living/dining space.

Nelson: Do you scrutinize other people's kitchens when you're in their homes?

Kate: A little—it depends on the person and my expectations of their kitchen! (She laughs)

Nelson: It's said that the kitchen is the heart of a home. Why do so many of us feel that way?

Kate: It's a shared space centered around food, so everyone is going to be in the kitchen. It's basically the only space in a home that everyone has to use at some point (unless you only have one bathroom). And (hopefully) it's filled with delicious things and smells, and who wouldn't want to be there?

Nelson: As written on the old tea towel, "No matter where I serve my guests, it seems they like my kitchen best!" (laughter). But seriously . . . there can't be a dream home without a dream kitchen. What would you tell someone are the essentials for making that come to life, even on a fixed/ modest budget?

Kate: Think hard about how you to like to cook and eat. For instance, some folks shop daily for food, so perhaps they need less pantry storage and a small fridge. Some people are very gadget-driven—if so, make sure there is ample space for the air fryer and slow cooker and pressure cooker, etc. I do think it's worth investing in a great range (it doesn't have to be enormous to be awesome). Also, countertops and backsplashes don't have to be expensive to be super nice looking and they can make such a difference in the look and feel of a space.

Nelson: Do you have any favorite kitchen resource guides you can share?

Kate: I like Houzz.com* a lot when it comes to getting inspired.

(*A great recommendation from Kate. Check it out, if you're not familiar with it!)

Nelson: What item would most surprise us to find in your fridge or pantry?

Kate: Hmmm. Not one but two boxes of Mallomars? (They're only in season for a short time!) Or maybe boxed mac and cheese? I think it's so good and so much easier to make than from scratch.

Nelson: Some people peek in medicine chests. Do you peek into fridges?

Kate: Only after three glasses of wine. (laughter)

Nelson: If you could visit anyone's kitchen (living or dead), whose would it be?

Kate: Julia Child or James Beard.

The Living Room (aka the Great Room)

Dominating the room is the Poliform wall system, which had been a hard sell for me considering the price tag. They tout themselves as "one of the most important companies in the world of international furniture for design quality, project excellence and innovation." I was skeptical, but was outvoted and, eventually, very glad I was. It somehow anchors this massive room without overpowering it, provides a showcase for so many of our treasures, and has alluring LED lighting that can only be described as sexy! It now houses some of our favorite books and individual family keepsakes, like my mother's serpentine sculpture of the goddess Niobi, an hourglass and an unusual antique Chinese carafe, whose handle is a slithering snake. Smack dab in the center of the Poliform is our largest Tobiasse painting, Bethsabee, so the entire unit almost serves as its wall-sized frame.

Jonny's prized *Circle of Life* sculpture by Tolla is the only object we have placed in front of the window, but its wide circular design seems to enhance the view rather than obstruct it.

Our Little Petra chair and ottoman from the Danish design company, & Tradition, turned out prettier than I imagined when Rebecca first showed it to us in the Suite NY showroom. Contemporary, comfy and an absolutely perfect complement to the wall coverings and flooring, its unique shape is covered in a neutral tweed fabric and customized with contrasting orange

buttons. Rebecca notes, "The complexity of the texture and colors in the tweed are enjoyed up close, and the buttons catch your eye from across the room." Swellegant, indeed!

Its cozy cousin is the Elysia Lounge Chair with ottoman, a deep rust color and, despite its geometric design, surprisingly plush and comfortable. With its Danish oiled wood frame, it gives a much more formal appearance than your bottom would expect when it sinks into the cushioning. If you're shopping for furniture you expect to spend a lot of time sitting in/on, it's always a smart idea to give it a test spin in the showroom. Rebecca and I spent many hours wiggling our bottoms onto various chairs, sofas and stools!

An electrical junction box (J Box) was rigged, allowing us to create a rope of light from Luke Lamp Company draped over a suspended bar. It is unusual, eye-catching and glows like Wonder Woman's magic lasso.

A small, modern bench is opposite the sofa with a cozy cashmere throw and is a sweet spot to sit and gaze out over the views of Harlem.

Centered among the furniture is our bespoke John Houshmand coffee table. Jonny had owned one of his pieces and it's a showstopper but was about six inches too low to work with the sofa and chairs. I campaigned to have Mr. Houshmand create a new base for it that would lift it to a better height, but the costs involved prompted us to opt for an entirely new piece. The first step of the process was to visit his design studio upstate in the Catskills, a three-hour drive north of the City. Rebecca made a day trip out of it and took videos of all our different fresh-cut wood choices (iPhones are a godsend for this kind of thing). We settled on a large log of spalted (deteriorating) maple that was then treated and shaped for us, before being cunningly mounted on a base and topped with glass. Not only one of a kind, but a breathtaking bit of nature right in the middle of our urban aerie. The customer service was unfortunately not as first-rate as the artistry but ultimately worth the wait.

The Dining Alcove

This gorgeous, light-filled corner of the great room was a tiny second bedroom in the original floorplan design. By opening it up, we were able to dramatically increase the size of the room and the expanse of the windows, views and natural light. Anything less would seem claustrophobic by comparison (rumor has it that other residents of the building have heard what we did and followed suit. Unfortunately for them, they had to tear down walls rather than not have them erected in the first place. Sometimes, the early bird catches the worm). It also left us with a structural pillar which not only adds a unique, industrial flair to the architecture of the room, but an interesting space on which to hang more art (a framed sculptural relief by Pier Monaghan) and some sconces to match the nearby Bocci chandelier.

Rebecca cleverly chose a stand-alone almost-golden wall covering for the pillar with a divine, shimmering texture. The two other Tobiasse paintings, *La Fiancee d'arlequin* and *Isaac et Rebecca,* hang here. On the window ledge we placed Jim Rennert's steel sculpture, *A Step Ahead,* which depicts a small "everyman" trying to keep from being rolled over by a giant circle/wheel. The geometry of the piece works beautifully with that of the windows, without obstructing any of the view. Nearby is a framed wooden sculpture of a Chinese jacket by Sun Yi . . . a real conversation piece. When dining out, Jonny and I often like to sit side-by-side. It feels right to us as a couple and we have the added bonus of both being able to

people watch. We wanted to create that restaurant dynamic here, so we had a specially built banquette created to fit into the corner of this room. It can easily accommodate four people and then we added two modern chairs opposite a large, round marble table. It was a testament to the craftsmanship of Rebecca's design, with the millworker's execution and the upholsterer's skill to bring it all together. Sitting in the exquisite banquette, one can enjoy a view of the Great Room or the long sweep of northern exposure overlooking the George Washington Bridge and the historic City College of New York. I challenge you to find a lovelier table with a better view in all of Manhattan. It definitely makes the case for "Eating In." It quickly became our preferred spot for morning coffee together, and often, we grab our laptops and do some work here, too.

Here is another Lucy Tupo custom rug, of the same color scheme as the foyer, but this one has an unusual "amoeba" shape that looks divine beneath the black Saarinen marble dining table and atop the light wooden floor. Keeping with our geometric patterns, David Kimball Anderson's steel sculpture Briar Berries, sits strikingly atop the banquette ledge.

The Bedroom

There's no other way to say it. It's small! Our queen-sized Charles bed from B&B Italia takes up most of the room, so we had to be dutiful about selecting the right nightstand tables, lest we fill up the entire room with bedding. Allied Maker sconces on both sides of the bed allow each of us to control our lighting and customizing the two closets for maximum efficiency was vital. A small but chic leather and bronze bureau from BDDW is opposite the bed and an adjacent linen closet, and that's it for this room! A flat-screen TV is mounted for morning news and occasionally evening entertainment—if we can manage to stay awake long enough.

However, if there's any space that works being small, it's the bedroom. We wanted a "cave" where we could nestle in for quality rest. Jonny could sleep through World War Three and cherishes any and every opportunity to close his eyes, but I am a dreadful sleeper and can rarely manage to get more than a couple solid hours of sleep at a time. Heavy blackout curtains help us close ourselves off from the rest of the world when we're in this room, even though we can take two steps up and open a door to our scenic terrace. It's great in the mornings, as the first light over the East River bathes us in sunshine . . . but at night, it's, "Do Not Disturb." Luxurious bedding and quality pillows help ensure that this room is truly an oasis for relaxation and rejuvenation. That's important for any bedroom.

The wall coverings in here are so light, lovely and subtle that you might not even notice the pattern until you look closely. Overhead, we have a sleek, taupe wall covering on the ceiling. It has a subtle sheen to it that is insanely elegant. The darker tones may subliminally lower the ceiling a bit, but it adds to the nest-like quality of the room. It was a stroke of design genius on Rebecca's part and perfectly frames a dramatic, block light fixture from Fuse Lighting. Over the bed, we have hung a wonderful winter photo of a Central Park sledding scene taken by talented Susan Wides. There are also three black and white photos of Paris (a special place to us) by Craig Sterling.

In this room you will find the only personal photos we have chosen to display. We both have large families of friends and relatives so there would be no way to include everyone, hence we made a very conscious choice about what photographs we would include in our décor. And we decided that they should all be cohesive in style and theme; Lord knows we had zillions from which to choose. We selected one photo of my parents, decked out in their most glamorous 1970s style on a cruise to Bermuda. Then one of Jonny's parents, all smiles, circa mid-80s. And finally, a shot of Jonny and me from 2019, onstage at the Perth Telethon in Australia. Three happy couples in their primes.

The Main Bathroom

Formerly known in real estate circles as the "Master Bathroom," (considered sexist?) the Main Bathroom has a large, glass walk-in shower with rainfall shower head, and built-in shelf for soaps and shampoo. White marble tiles on the walls and double vanity perfectly match the grey chevron tiles on the floor. Deep, deep drawers provide unexpected, ample storage space. A brightly lighted, double-sized, mirrored medicine chest features lights and electrical outlets inside as well. It is a simple but elegant sanctuary for our "Master," Jonny. Black matte fixtures and hooks throughout.

On the large wall opposite the mirrors are ten multicolored, ceramic Jacks and two red balls (who remembers playing that game as a kid?) which add color and levity to the otherwise elegant setting. Rebecca cleverly selected bright, matching bath linens to further accentuate them.

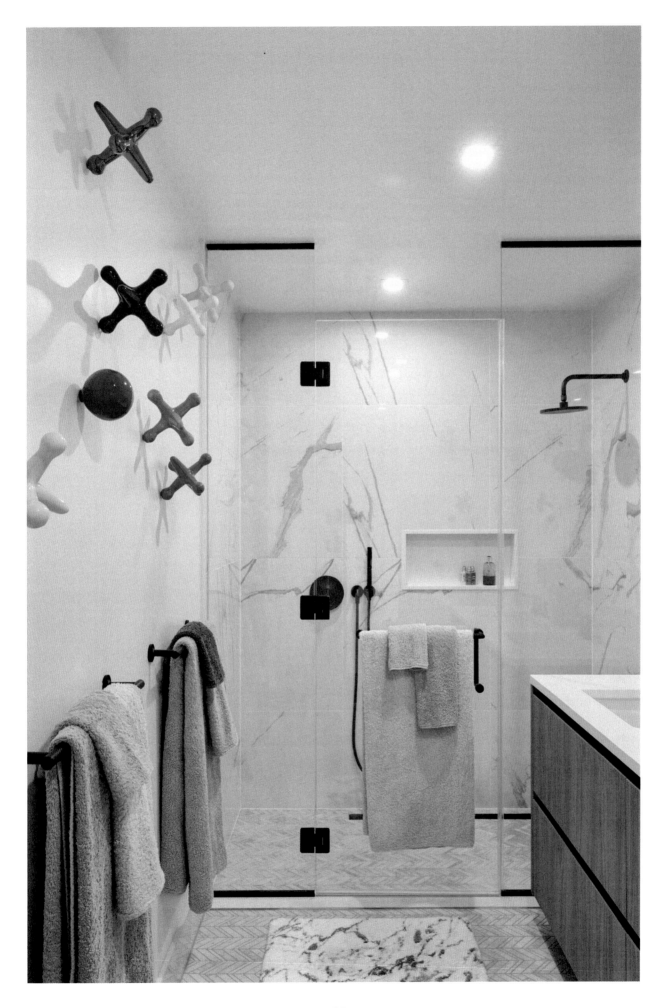

The Secondary Bathroom

This is my "workspace" for when I have to get camera-ready for my job. It's also a large, luxurious bathroom with the exact same tiles and fixtures as the Main Bathroom (we had the option from the building developers of having a different design, but I liked the idea of continuity). A real indulgence is that the floor tiles in this room are heated. I swapped out the double vanity for a single one—and subsequent smaller medicine chest— so that I'd have a little more elbow room in there. If a future owner wanted to reinstall a double vanity, all the plumbing is there for an easy swap. A full tub and shower with rainfall shower head and detachable spray hose is accessed through a glass half-door. In addition to adding some extra hooks for sweaty running gear, I also had two grab bars installed for any future trouble I may have getting in and out. Meantime, they're extra towel racks! An extendable magnifying mirror attached to the generous, lighted medicine chest is a bonus.

This personal pocket of the home is mine, all mine, so I do have some very special belongings there that don't need to be shared with the more trafficked spaces. Tucked away are some novelty items that amuse me tremendously: a statue fragment of a foot, uncovered by my parents in the early 1960s when they excavated their farm . . . a bronze death mask of my face made for me by artist Philip Hitchcock and permanently preserves how I looked in 1995 (I have it hung over the toilet and I do get a kick out of telling people, "It's the king on his throne,") . . . and a magnificent Iranian rug I've been preserving in storage for so long that I finally decided, "What am I saving it for?" It's extremely luxurious to have this underfoot while padding around in there.

On the walls opposite the shower is a woodcutting print, *Morning Snow* by NYC artist Ellen Nathan Singer and two ultra-mid-century modern oil paintings by an unknown artist, painted in 1963. These small, unframed beauties depict the medieval city of Ferarra in northeast Italy, situated on the River Po, about fifty kilometers northeast of Bologna. The colors are muted greens, blues and pinks, as serene as I imagine the setting to be. As a lover of Tuscany, I have never traveled that far north in Italy before, so these lovely works are a constant reminder for me to always keep exploring new places.

The Laundry Room

The unit we originally wanted to purchase did not have a laundry room, but instead a small closet with a stackable washer and dryer. While we gave up a narrow little spiral stairway to the rooftop cabana, this unit afforded us a high-ceilinged full room not only for the appliances but precious storage space for household cleaning equipment, laundry detergent and the like. Our designer, together with a mill worker, made a beautiful, pleasant space in which to tend to the washing. We even have a drop-down ironing board and built-in hamper to maximize space efficiency. An eye-catching Venice Terrazzo countertop from Concrete Collaborative completes the bright, airy look of this gem of a room. A small Verner Panton mustard-colored lamp adds ambiance where you'd least expect it. I knew I would be spending tons of time there (I love doing laundry) so it was important to make it aesthetically appealing as well as functionally efficient.

In the vestibule outside the laundry room, connecting the western rooms to the Great Room, we painted the ceiling in sky-blue lacquer to make it seem even higher, and it reflects the handsome Allied Maker light fixture so that it provides twice the beauty. The color provides a subtle connection to the blue hues in the adjacent rooms' artworks.

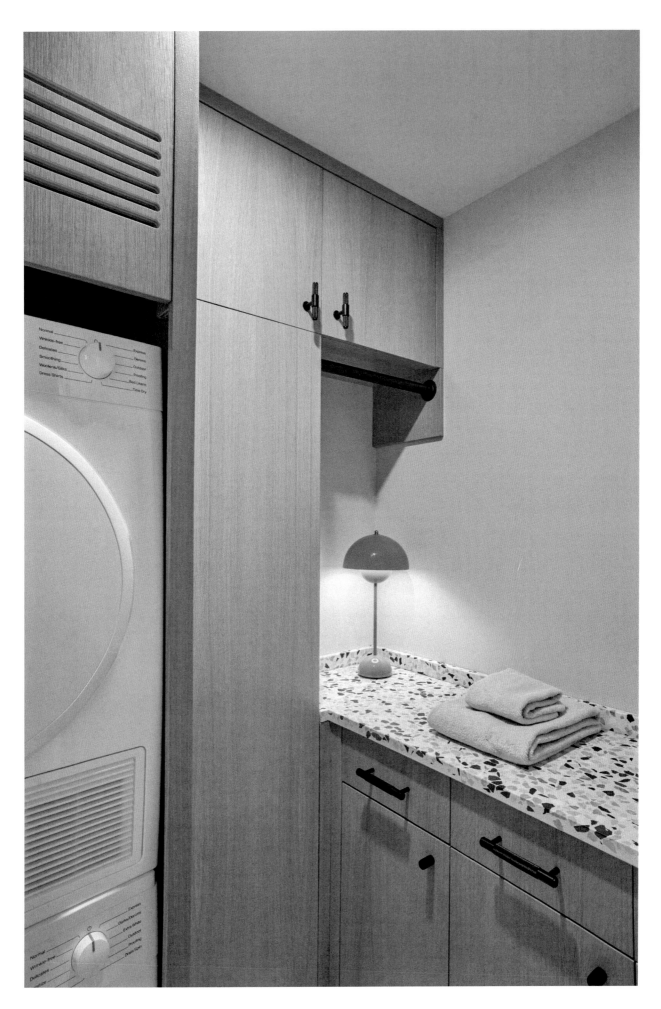

The Office

After two years of a pandemic necessitated working from home, I wanted us to have the most stunning and comfortable office space possible. Jonny and I are both borderline workaholics and, given our international jobs and the advent of staying constantly electronically connected, we are pretty much on call around the clock and we log in long work hours. An office where we would spend so much time, often together, would have to be a pleasant place.

My previous workspace, though larger, was a cluttered and miserable room full of TV production equipment including an eight-foot-high green screen, two tripods with ring lights, additional light projectors, microphones, cameras and recording equipment. Anyone who believes in feng shui would have had a heart attack looking at that mess. Every day for nearly twenty-four months, I navigated my way through it all to keep broadcasting to my audience—even with the unflattering makeshift lighting and camera quality.

Here, our thoughtfully designed closets neatly house all my equipment and our office supplies, and Rebecca designed an incredible L-shaped desk where Jonny and I could work side by side. The desk itself is very minimalist with floating drawers, and it's topped with a lovely smoked glass, so we don't lose any of our gorgeous window views that stretch to the north and west. Simple shades are available, both opaque, to cut any glare and create total black out for when I need to broadcast.

On the opposite wall, we created a comfy, overstuffed Montauk Sofa with storage room underneath. This is where we can snuggle up and watch the television which we had mounted on an extension arm for when we're finally able to switch off from work duties. An incredible wall covering includes black, gray newsprint (in a nod to my work as a journalist) and hint of orange. The sofa pillows have orange piping to offset the plain but handsome beige color, and our straight-back desk chairs are also upholstered in a dark orange fabric. There is an interesting architectural feature in the northwest corner of this room: a broad column we painted in a stunning orange lacquer (a zillion coats required!). Hanging over the sofa is our large, cheerful and colorful Jane Waterous oil painting, Circle of Life, that's actually four separate panels (more on that later). An orange lacquered side table from DOT is just right for setting down a beverage and the remote control.

If you can pull your gaze away from the breathtaking views, you'll see one of my favorite features of this room—the great, glass globe pendant light hanging overhead from a small chain. In tones of orange and grey, Rebecca conceived the design and worked with Brooklyn's Avram Rusu and Keep Handmade Glass Lighting to craft her vision to life. It was amazing to watch a simple nub of glass become a work of art that also provides a light source. Watching the artisans in their studio was awe inspiring and too irresistible for me not to post on Instagram.

It is always a challenge for me to keep my desk unfettered but, other than my laptop, a calculator and my daily diary, the only objects you will find there are my 2020 Publicists Guild International Media Award, my Golden Bobblehead likeness from when The Wiggles made me an honorary member of the band, and a perfectly smoothed stone from the rocky Montauk Point State Park beach where I had a special excursion with my best friend.

Three possessions of which I am especially proud and enjoy seeing during the course of my day. Jonny keeps a retro, bright orange rotary dial telephone on his side of the desk. It's definitely a conversation piece and it constantly surprises me how many people have never seen one.

The Terrace

Even though this is an outside space, it seems like the best room in the house! Stretching the length of the dining room and bedroom, this large rectangle has nothing but open sky overhead and an amazing view stretching from the George Washington Bridge to the north, past the iconic Apollo Theater marquee all the way to the East River. We wanted to landscape it simply but lushly so wherever you were inside you could enjoy the great outdoors. Inexpensive, interlocking wood pavers went over the cement and Franz James' local floral boutique did an outstanding job installing planters with hearty, low maintenance greenery (Euonymus, Juniper and Boxwoods) mimicking the style of our building's entry, creating a sense of thematic flow from street level to penthouse. A simple irrigation system and subtle lighting on timers make it simultaneously easy and elegant. (We had all this work executed early on to avoid any indoor mess, and Franz comes seasonally to freshen up the planters.) A six-foot Japanese maple in a large, square black planter brings us immense pleasure, especially when its delicate red leaves dance in the wind.

We don't use the outside area as often as we should, even though it's easily accessible through doors in the Great Room and the bedroom and has an electric heater installed to extend the al fresco opportunities all year long. Two industrial looking all-weather chairs with a small circular table are our preferred spots for morning juices or evening libations. But we enjoy its expansive beauty from almost everywhere in the home, every day. Not only gorgeous to behold, having outdoor space visible from inside the home can make even a modest-sized abode look huge. The next plan is to find some beautiful pots for perennials and maybe even an herb garden. Rosemary and basil are my go-to favorites for beautiful, fragrant plants that also comes in handy for cooking.

Sunrise, Sunset isn't just a song from *Fiddler on the Roof.* They're the times of day that are breathtaking to drink in and a regular reminder for us to count our many blessings.

The Cabana

This should be subtitled *The NeverEnding Story* because, as of this writing, its design is still evolving. Burned out on construction, we put the kibosh on a pergola and are instead opting for a large, cantilever umbrella to combat the rooftop's all-day exposure to full sunlight. This wide deck with its 360° city views will surely be our go-to entertaining space, complete with a built-in gas grill, sink, mini-fridge and storage. Privacy fences separate each cabana from our neighbors (Mother always said, "Good fences make good neighbors."). They also provide chic uniformity for aesthetics and a modicum of security. We selected Harbour Outdoor furniture from Australia that is weather resistant and comfortable. Franz James replicated our terrace planters and added a stunning Japanese maple (a design promptly copied by one of our neighbors. I suppose "imitation is the sincerest form of flattery!"). A self-timed irrigation and lighting system saves us from having to schlep up there on days we aren't using the space.

A note on fencing: if you're adding this feature to your outdoor space make sure to keep it appropriate to the size and scale of the space. Your home may be your castle, but that doesn't mean you should build fortress-sized walls.

Now that you've been through our house, I have included a design specific Q&A with Rebecca which may help guide and inspire you on your journey.

Nelson: In a world inundated with "DIY," when should a person call in professional design help?

Rebecca: The concept of home design has grown exponentially in the last ten to fifteen years with the proliferation of things like HGTV, Pinterest, Houzz and countless design books and magazines. People increasingly appreciate a well-appointed and well-functioning home. The pandemic amplified this understanding of the importance of our homes as a space where we live, relax, play, entertain and possibly work, and each of those things requires different solutions.

Some people have a natural "eye" and feel comfortable pulling a room together. It takes knowing yourself and your needs and a degree of confidence to do this. For those less confident but willing to try, the above-mentioned resources offer great inspiration to use as a starting point. Save images of what you like and note why—do you like specific furnishings or wallcoverings, or a light fixture, or is it the combination of colors or textures, or a unique mix of eclectic findings? Understanding why you like something is important—it frees you to find a similar solution in a broader pool of options. If it is the contrasting citron pillows on a plum sofa, you can hone your search to a specific color while being open to lots of textures. Likewise, if you know you like the warm, fuzzy feeling in a good reading nook chair, you've narrowed your scope to a specific texture but may find a lot of options across different styles and budgets.

Nelson: So, when should someone consider hiring a designer?

Rebecca: Simply stated, a designer takes into account all the details that make a difference in a project. They think through the details of function, circulation, style and scale of furnishings, textures and colors, lighting, and so much more. A designer will take the time to know you, understand your needs, examine and measure the space, discuss budget and help prioritize the work. I had a client who had purchased all his furnishings from a well-known home furnishing chain, and he had spent tens of thousands on the effort. The result was that his home lacked his family's personality — it closely resembled a showroom vignette. Additionally, many of the pieces were oversized for his space and he had too many furnishings, so the space didn't function as needed. He hired Method + Moxie to come up with a new vision that would meet his family's needs and support all the functions that home needed to serve for each of them. We met with the entire family together and individually to understand their needs and personalities so we could pull together a custom curated portfolio of furnishings and other finishes (some existing, some new) that would meet their requirements. Their investment resulted in a home that reflects their family's personality and style and provides a better functioning environment — and it saved them from making incorrect purchases they would have to abandon and replace.

Nelson: Finding the right designer might seem overwhelming. What's the best way to get started?

Rebecca: Before you look for a designer, have a good sense of your scope of work and budget for the project. Word of mouth is always a good option, but lacking that, probably the most prolific platforms showcasing designers are Houzz and Pinterest. Local magazines are a good resource as well for local designers, and if you are purchasing a new home your realtor is likely connected to some designers. Designing a residential space is very personal, and so it's important to find someone you not only trust as a qualified design professional, but someone you will enjoy working with. It's a relationship, and hopefully one that lasts a very long time and over many projects. So, take the time to meet with the designer, understand their process, look at their portfolio or website, potentially ask for references and definitely understand their billing methodology. Interview a few to find the right fit.

Nelson: Budgets are challenging. What do you suggest prioritizing (financially) when beginning a design project?

Rebecca: All clients have budgets. Even if they are wildly large budgets, most people place more value on some items than others and prefer to invest more in certain rooms or specific pieces. In my experience, most who are diving into a project for the first time aren't familiar enough with the wide array of options and associated costs to define a dollar amount up front. Whether you are working with a designer or not, it's beneficial to know what you're willing to spend on a project before you get started. It will help you and the designer prioritize very early on in the process and will save a lot of time (and money!) that is otherwise wasted looking in the wrong place for items. If you are tackling the project on your own, consider where you spend the most amount of time, and then what you need to address so it functions as you need it to. For instance, if you are focused on a family room and need a really comfortable sofa that will seat six, find a sectional you love and budget for that first, then allocate the budget across the other items. Also — if you're patient and can take a longer-term approach, the entire room needn't be completed at once. Leverage some existing pieces until you can add in other items you like.

Nelson: What's the most common design mistake you see?

Rebecca: Lighting is probably the most important element in a room and often the least considered one. As we have transitioned into a new language of lighting in recent years, from the old familiar incandescent wattage that was universally understood, the mistakes can be easily compounded.

First you want to make sure you have sufficient lighting. Poor lighting can ruin the appeal of an otherwise brilliant room. Create layers of lighting to accommodate the different functions a room needs to fulfill. Overhead lighting or sufficient lamp lighting (if overhead is not an option) offers broad light across a space. Task lighting for desk or other work areas will ensure you have enough lighting to tackle more detailed tasks. And ambient lighting can fill in gaps, soften corners and provide a nice evening lighting option for a more relaxed vibe.

Second, LEDs have become more prevalent and while more expensive, are far more energy efficient so you won't have to replace bulbs often.

LEDs offer an array of color temperatures (and colors if that's your thing) and these are very important to understand when purchasing bulbs. I would recommend always buying dimmable because it's nice to have the option (dimming switch required), and then understand that warmer hues (2700k–3000k) are most typical for residential use, with the lower number being a warmer, more golden undertone. As you go higher in the kelvin scale to 4500–5000k these are considered daylight and have a harsh, white tone to them. Perhaps fine for office work during daylight hours, but not relaxing at all when your body wants to naturally start winding down and preparing for rest at the end of a day.

Nelson: What's the best investment a person can make when creating their dream space?

Rebecca: If you're just starting down the path of designing a new space, the largest pieces will garner the most attention so I would focus on investing in a sofa and bed that you love. The coordinating pieces, end tables, accessories are easy to fill in and can be more easily changed out over time. If you have these pieces you love, then my preference would be to find some really fun lighting to bring into the room—something that can be the focal point of the room. There are so many great options to choose from at all budget levels, and it can be a simple way to bring in a lot more light.

Nelson: Who is the most difficult kind of client?

Rebecca: The easiest clients to work with are decisive. They have clear opinions on what they like and don't like. It saves time and gives us direction. We are working with a client now who from the start declared that she hated brown and straight lines, so we have clear direction on palette and geometries, and we follow those patterns in specifying many details, including hardware and lighting elements.

Nelson: What would be the most important component of your dream home?

Rebecca: Color. I love color. Not in an overwhelming way, but rather in a neutral and comfortable surrounding that lets me imbibe some vitality through pops of color. I love a livable, contemporary, clean-lined vibe with playful elements and lots of color.

Nelson: If a couple disagrees on a design choice, how do you recommend compromise?

Rebecca: There is always a reason for a design choice, and the logic for that selection should be explainable. So first understand the reason something was selected. If it's as simple as a client dislikes a choice, there are always other options, and I would seek to find another option both clients love. As in love, there is never just one perfect match!

Who's Zooming Whom?

Over the course of my quarter century of working in morning television,
I've interviewed literally thousands of celebrities in settings as
wide ranging as red carpets and hotel suites, to movie set locations and
their homes or dressing rooms. I always try to be as prepared as possible
and ready not only with intelligent, insightful questions but the capacity to
really listen to what they have to say in response and react/follow through
appropriately. It's not unusual to find a movie star who doesn't listen*,
but you'd be surprised how many "journalists" actually don't! In 2020, I
was honored to receive the International Media Award from the esteemed
Publicists Guild of America in 2020 as well as invited to join the Critics
Choice Association, so my access to A-List interviews is not a responsibility
I take lightly, whether it's scaling a Manhattan skyscraper alongside
Martina Navritolova or having a bit of fun in the kitchen with Meryl Streep
or Harrison Ford.

*Exceptions to this are Keanu Reeves, Rita Moreno, Julianne Moore, Jeff
Goldblum and Joseph Gordon-Levitt. They never miss a trick and really
pay attention to the question before formulating wonderful answers.

I've always been a "fanboi," but that doesn't mean I can afford the luxury
of being star struck. My very first celebrity-related assignment was to

train Princess Diana in the hot new workout of 1990: Step Aerobics. No room for cold feet there. As it turned out, by the time I got to London, royal protocol dictated that I would instead train her trainer, but the subsequent television exposure I enjoyed led directly to my long career in "breakfast TV." You'd think I might get nervous going into Betty White's living room or singing on stage alongside Hugh Jackman, but I learned from an acting teacher a long time ago that when you feel like you might get overwhelmed by nerves, just embrace it as a sign that you care greatly about the task at hand. The same advice could be applied to anything that produces anxiety (including home renovation or design!).

When Covid-19 all but shut down showbiz production in the spring of 2020, the promotional wheels didn't stop turning. The entertainment industry carried on through the miracle of modern technology to complete and release hundreds of projects that were "in the queue." But instead of my usual jetsetting every week or two for the subsequent interviews and press tours, the world abruptly shifted to Zoom meetings and Skype calls. Even my daily news reports were jettisoned from the comfort of a TV studio with flattering lighting, flawless satellite connections and professional engineering and relegated to my little iPhone with a ring light and a cumbersome green screen that made me look a bit gruesome. My vanity took a hit, but at least I was able to keep working. This was a turning point for millions of employees around the world who suddenly found themselves working remotely from home. Personally, I hate it. The commute may be a breeze, but it's almost impossible to ever "call it a day" and switch off. Nor am I a Gadget Guy. Technology comes neither easily nor naturally to me. You'll notice I haven't mentioned a sophisticated sound system in our new home, but it remains at the top of our priority list. They key for us will be to keep it "dummy-proof!"

The stars had to pivot as well. Celebrities who were accustomed to private jets, fancy suites, catering and a coterie of groomers, stylists and press agents now had to figure out how to upload and use Webex to fulfill their PR duties. Some succeed better than others. Poor Julia Stiles recently dialed in from somewhere in Canada and looked like she was calling from inside a burning building! Honestly, while I missed the glamour of jetting off to Cannes or Hollywood for a celebrity chat, I find that the conversations can be more relaxed and revealing when you are speaking to them from the comfort of their own homes. During a recent interview with Broadway impresario Lin-Manuel Miranda from his apartment just up the street in Washington Heights, he spontaneously thought of something he wanted to show me and jumped up to retrieve it, hopping right over the couch in the process. It was a charming, candid moment that would never have happened within the confines of a studio.

Even some of the most die-hard Tinseltown types decided to downsize. The talented and genetically blessed couple Justin Timberlake and Jessica Biel put their massive, ten-acre Spanish Villa style estate on the market in October of 2021, after deciding they no longer needed seven bedrooms, a gym, a screening room, an outdoor entertaining space wrapping around the entire house, a separate guest house, tennis court and twenty-five-meter pool. Listed at $48 million, it shows that even after a pandemic the Hollywood Hills are still a sought-after destination: they bought the property in 2002 for "only" $8.3 million.

In another pandemic shift, Neil Patrick Harris and his family finally found a buyer for their massive and impeccably renovated Harlem NYC brownstone, which dates back to 1908. Offered at $7,325,000, they took $7.1 for the light-filled, six-story Italian style residence which also features two thousand square feet of outdoor space and a subterranean movie theater. It's a record for the neighborhood and proves that the future of Manhattan is heading northward. Famous for their elaborate Christmas decorations that have lighted up the block every December since 2013, Neil and his husband will surely miss the convenience of city dwelling the next time they're appearing on Broadway . . . but I guess at those prices, a limo drive or helicopter hop in from the Hamptons isn't too unbearable. But for every departure, there is an arrival. No sooner did Neil split than journalist Soledad O'Brien and her family plopped down $4.95 million for a six bedroom, newly renovated Harlem penthouse.

If you're reliant on virtual meetings, now more than ever you have the technical wherewithal to ensure good lighting but also give thought to the background in which your colleagues see you. You're essentially having them over to your home, so make sure it is clean and inviting. For most of 2020 and 2021, I did my interviews from inside my home office, which is adorned with an Indonesian war shield (it looks a bit like a big surfboard!) and a whimsical paneled oil painting by Canadian artist Jane Waterous. It's interesting and offers color and depth to the "shot" without stealing focus. (That said, Sandra Oh, Ray Liotta, Kyle Richards and Jimmy Smits all wanted to talk more about my artwork than they did about their film projects!)

The last in-person celebrity interview I did before lockdown was with the ubiquitous Australian actress Rose Byrne. We'd had many interviews in the past, so there was usually a hug upon arrival but already by the end of February 2020, everyone had switched to socially distant fist-bumps instead. (Jake Gyllenhall has always been known as a germaphobe and often had an excuse ready to avoid handshakes, so this scenario was a welcome change!) Rose was out to promote a film whose release would consequently be delayed by a year and, much like Daniel Craig's final outing as 007 in *No Time to Die* lost its momentum as cinemas around the world shuttered. But it wasn't long before Zoom junkets became the new normal and my first "customer" was the fabulous and funny Traci Ellis Ross, chatting from her place in the Hollywood Hills. I was actually conducting my side of the interview from my location in my best friend's beautiful Hamptons house where I spent ten full weeks of quarantine without missing a day of work (five of us and a French bulldog stayed out there the entire time and managed not to kill each other. Facetime sessions with your therapist are genius!).

The last celebrity hug I received before lockdown was from Jennifer Aniston—a good one to get, if you only get one! She was a presenter at the Publicists Guild Awards and was backstage when I came off from accepting my trophy. I was so elated, I just had to hug someone, and she was there and didn't mind at all! She gave me a big congrats, which was especially appreciated since I've interviewed her so many times over the years and our long history goes all the way back to the early 1980s when I worked with her dad, John Aniston, on the long running soap opera *Search for Tomorrow.* Jennifer actually auditioned for a role on that show to play a teenage runaway named T.R. (for Teenage Runaway . . . how original!) but lost out to darling Jane Krakowski, who would win an Emmy for her performance. Jane was perfect on *30 Rock* and only Jennifer could have played Rachel on *Friends,* so I guess everything worked out the way it was supposed to! By the way, the best hugger in showbiz is—hands down—Queen Latifah! Camila Cabello would be a close second and I've interviewed her so many times that our chats always begin and end with her giving her "Uncle Nelson" a big embrace.

The more you Zoom, the easier it gets. I think we all learned that over the course of the pandemic, whether it was Home Schooling, Holiday Gatherings or Work Meetings. I even, sadly, attended a friend's Zoom funeral . . . a surreal experience, but in hindsight a blessing that we were all able to share our memories of the deceased, simultaneously. I think Jennifer Hudson must spend a lot of time chatting with friends and family over Zoom, because she is as natural and easy-going as if she were right

there in the room with you. She is always dazzling with her enthusiasm and insight, and always quick to share her musical gifts; she might just spontaneously burst into song at any moment. And you sure are lucky when she does!

No matter how tech savvy or camera-friendly, some folks just can't figure out "eye lines" and remember to look directly into the camera lens. Surprisingly, it's often the younger subjects who seem to be gazing off into space even though they're actually looking at the image of me they see on their screens. It is worth investing in a good camera and lighting if you can come out looking like Chris Pratt, Jessica Biel or Julianne Moore. Be flexible about distractions, interruptions and technical glitches . . . that's par for the course with new technology. Poor Awkwafina had to redo our entire interview when her side failed to record—but she did a complete second take with as much energy and spontaneity as the first time. Sirens blaring from the street and ringing phones may sometimes break the flow of conversation, but they also provide a healthy dose of reality often absent from celebrity interviews. The incessant squawking of Hilary Swank's exotic pet bird was coming from off-camera, so I had to acknowledge it and then the bird became a part of the interview, and it was a ton of fun!

Julianne told me how, during lockdown, she'd recorded her entire vocal performance for the animated film, *Spirit Untamed*, from the solitude of her little laundry room, with towels stuffed under the door to muffle the sounds of her dogs barking outside. Charlize Theron didn't mind voicing her Morticia character in the *Addams Family* animated sequel from home.

Her kids got to play the other parts while she recorded her lines (I'm sure she missed driving to and from the studio — she has confessed to me that "alone time" in the car is precious to her!).

Two masters of interviews, virtual or otherwise, are George Clooney and Hugh Jackman. No two stars are more charismatic, gracious and well spoken, regardless of the situation. While George told me he lamented the change saying, "These Zoom things are ridiculous. Won't it be nicer when we can all be in the same room again?" But I got him to admit that there was the bright side of not having to constantly stop for selfies with all his many admirers. Hugh, too, claims to miss the personal interaction, even with journalists. I reminded him that at least it gives him a rest from Barista duties: often when he hosts a press day, he brings all the equipment to whip up custom made drinks made from his own coffee label, Laughing Man.

By the end of 2021, everyone pretty much had the hang of it all and stopped making jokes about whatever they were (or were not) wearing from the waist down. On a related note, my first in-person interview after the pandemic was with pop sensation Shawn Mendes, when I was invited to spend the afternoon with him at his glorious Malibu mountaintop retreat. Maybe it was inspired by too many Zoom calls, but he spent the first hour I was there walking around in only his underwear while we set up the cameras. Maybe he wanted to show off his impressive physique or maybe he's just that comfortable in his own skin. I know Lizzo is: when I interviewed her, she wasn't wearing anything at all below the waist! The cameraman was diligent about keeping the shot strictly on her clothed upper half!

Put Your Feet Up

When you are the King or Queen of your Castle, you are encouraged to put your feet up, relax and enjoy your domain! And if you're entertaining, make sure that everything is as sparkling as your guest list. Take an example from one of Hollywood's greatest hostesses, Joan Crawford, of whom Noel Coward once said, "Joan not only gives a party, she goes to it!" If you are prepared and relaxed, you should be able to enjoy yourself as much as your visitors. And no matter how elegant the setting, you must let people be themselves and have fun in the space. If you're too nervous about having them near the china cupboard, then move the activities to another part of your home where no one (especially you!) has to be self-conscious. (Our magnificent, textured wall coverings are almost irresistible to touch so we always "jokingly" welcome admiring guests by jovially saying, "Look but don't touch!" We mean it.)

Perfection is something many strive to achieve. Some do. But no one can sustain it. We found it to be a tremendous adjustment to live with those first scratches, stains, scuffs and smudges . . . much the same way a driver has to cope with the first dings on the car hood, or we adapt to new crinkles around our eyes. Take a deep breath and chill. A happy home is one that is "lived in" and one in which you feel at ease.

Just as Covid-19 threw our well-laid new home plans into chaos—along with almost every other aspect of modern life—we pivoted as needed and I think the ability to be flexible ultimately made things better for us. Literally the week we finally moved in, the Omicron variant was rearing its ugly head and new mandates were going into place almost daily. Whenever I felt frustrated by all the unexpected developments, I reminded myself that we don't have to put off our "Happily Ever Afters." You can decide to start yours anytime you want. How about today?

The Doctor is In: The Psychology of Creating Your Dream Home

––––––––––

It's easy to say that tackling a project like building, designing or renovating your space so that it will become a "dream home" can be daunting. And it's easy to offer advice with the caveat that it shouldn't be stressful. The reality is that, no matter how smoothly things go . . . no matter how carefully you preplan and execute your tasks . . . no matter how good natured you try to be, there will inevitably be frustrating and stressful snags along the way.

For us, we relied greatly on the advice and guidance of our design and development teams, but even if you're doing things on your own, I believe there is a psychology to it all—just as (or maybe more) valuable than your budget! Like a funeral, a pregnancy or a move, major life events can take a toll on the most solid of relationships or stoic personalities.

For my partner and me, the dreaded "Punch List" was a landmine of nerves and potential conflict. A Punch List, according to the Business Dictionary, is defined as "Listing of Items Requiring Immediate Attention" and as "a list of work that does not conform to contract specifications." In other words, or in our case, it was a mishmash of still-unfinished items from the time we signed off on purchasing our condo, at the closing. Whether you're working with a broker, developer, contractor or designer, it's always important to be clear about what things are still "To Be Done" and document them legally to ensure their completion. It can be anything from a scuff mark on a floorboard to a chipped piece of glass to more major issues like a missing door handle, incorrectly installed appliance or backwards hinge in a cabinet door. Nothing should be considered off limits, large or small, from including on your Punch List—as long as you make sure both parties agree to sign off on them before you seal the deal. (Fun fact: the term comes from the antiquated process of punching actual holes into a list to denote items that require repair.)

While Jonny's and my personalities are almost always in harmony, there can be times when we are complete opposites. It's kind of nice, in fact, because we can balance each other out in times of conflict. When one of us is alarmed or anxious, the other is the calming force. I'm also far less patient or confrontational, so far more inclined, for example, to let something slide while he is a persistent perfectionist, almost never willing to say, "that will be good enough." We found a way to play Good Cop/Bad Cop, which actually works beautifully in many aspects of our life. I tend to smile, cajole and entertain the troops while fielding offers, gathering options and weeding through any and all possibilities presented to us. I take these to him and then he, as the Bad Cop, can swoop in for a cameo appearance and decree the final decisions. Sometimes the roles reverse, but when it comes to domestic stuff, that is usually how it plays out. I think most couples who work well together have probably adopted a similar strategy to coping with life's challenges.

It got me thinking about the psychology involved with the whole process, so I consulted with a couple of friends who know a lot on that subject. Dr. Alan Steinberg works with individuals facing a wide range of issues including anxiety, depression, trauma, attentional disorders, impulse control and life transitions. I met with him to help me treat my insomnia. My dear friend Ilene V. Fishman, LCSW, is a psychotherapist and well-known expert on eating disorders and author of *The Deeper Fix*. She has also appeared on the hit show, *The Real Housewives of New Jersey* as a counselor.

Nelson: What are the psychological benefits of creating a dream home for yourself?

Dr. Steinberg: A dream home is a reflection of our inner self, a mirror of our inner core. A dream home reflects our emotional needs, our aspirations, inspirations, our values and importantly, our aesthetic self. The designs, colors, fabrics, textures, furniture styles, accessories and artwork we choose are projections of our personality. When our outer world aligns in meaningful ways with our inner world, it brings a deep sense of satisfaction, fulfillment and overall well-being.

Because a dream home reflects our inner selves, it manifests itself differently for different people. A cozy rustic log cabin in the woods can bring as much satisfaction to its owner as a sprawling luxury apartment in Manhattan can to its owner. What these two homes have in common is that they fulfill one's inner needs for an emotionally nourishing environment.

Home design can improve mental health. Many interior design elements have been shown to reduce anxiety, stress and depression. For example, most of us intuitively know that light, colors and art affect our mood. The connection between emotional well-being and interior design is well documented across decades of research from the fields of environmental psychology, interior design and architecture. Most importantly, as you prepare and shop for all the ingredients you'll need to furnish your new home, let your mood, your heart and your inner core guide you in your selections.

Be assured that the time, effort and money you put into your dream home will ultimately pay off—your dream home will nurture your soul.

Ilene V. Fishman: Our homes are an extension of our relationship with ourselves. As we grow, our homes come to represent where we are on our life journey. If we're lucky, we are able to externalize our personal development through our home creation. Even small decorating changes can express our current state of consciousness and being.

What makes us uncomfortable or comfortable? What colors, textures, fabrics, images feel right? What felt right then may not feel right now. How wonderful to be able to adjust, grow and change our surroundings!

Nelson: What are useful tools for dealing with the inevitable delays/ snafus/headaches involved with such a project?

Ilene V. Fishman: The better we know ourselves, the more we can curate our living space accordingly. Having just finished my first major home renovation, which I found full of strife and challenges, I am now on the other side and know firsthand the joy and feeling of accomplishment of being in a new personal space. I had to stretch myself and it was quite uncomfortable but ultimately worth it. The pandemic offered us new "eyes" as we spent more time than ever inside our homes. Our environmental comfort took on a whole new meaning. Home was no longer the place where we just touched base only to live our lives out in the world again. Our homes became our entire world.

Dr. Steinberg: I recommend a combination of tools—cognitive strategies and meditation/mindfulness exercises. While there are many different types of cognitive strategies, the ones I will focus on here are mindsets and expectations. Importantly, having a realistic mindset is key to helping you manage stress and disappointment. Keep in mind that a dream home does not equate to a perfect home. Perfection is unachievable, thus, expecting perfection will set you up for disappointment, frustration, anger and stress.

Be prepared to compromise. Know what you want, go for what you want, but be prepared to make adjustments during your journey. Oftentimes, the compromises you make will greatly diminish in importance after you start living in your dream home. However, if there are a select few design elements that you feel are non-negotiable, know what they are from the outset and protect them from any outside influences.

Another recommendation is to allow for disappointments along the way. Although disappointments are not inevitable, they are likely. When you encounter disappointment, acknowledge it and try to identify the specific feelings you're experiencing. Accept your feelings without judgment and allow yourself to move through the disappointment at your own pace. It's important to exercise patience with your emotions. Whatever you're feeling is okay, even if you feel you're overreacting. Disappointment fades with the passage of time. Acknowledging and validating your feelings like this will help you cope with the toughest moments in a healthy way.

While having a healthy and adaptable mindset will help you manage your stress, these strategies may not be sufficient to quell your stress response. You should have a few stress-reduction exercises on tap. Here are some suggestions:

Download an app that contains guided meditation for stress-reduction and/or mindfulness. Develop a healthy habit of daily practice. These exercises are most effective if they are practiced daily.

Mindfulness exercises typically include breathing meditations that focus on your breath, body scan meditations that focus on tension in your body. There are even meditations specifically designed to help you work with difficulties. Mindfulness can lower your stress level and gives you the space to respond calmly under pressure. It helps inhibit a stress response. It may help you develop a higher tolerance for sitting with uncomfortable feelings and a greater ability to process these feelings more effectively. Mindfulness can also improve your level of care and compassion for yourself.

Another common type of relaxation exercise focuses on deep breathing or diaphragmatic breathing. This technique involves deeper, slower breaths which can induce relaxation almost instantly. It's a simple exercise to try — inhale through your nose, count to eight and focus on drawing breath from your abdomen rather than your chest. Exhale slowly through your nose at the same pace, counting to eight. Complete this cycle a few times. You should notice a drop in your stress level, and perhaps a lowered heart rate as well.

Another common relaxation exercise is progressive muscle relaxation. Progressive muscle relaxation is an exercise that reduces stress in your body by having you slowly tense and then relax each muscle. This exercise can provide an immediate feeling of relaxation. Here too, it's best to practice this exercise frequently. With more experience, you will become more aware of when and where you are feeling tension and you will have the skills to help yourself relax.

Ilene V. Fishman: Play, have fun. Delight in your creativity. Be conscious regarding questions of seriousness in your design versus fun and whimsy. Be flexible with yourself. Try not to second-guess every decision (like me!). Live with your space so that you can patiently and more organically choose what you like and want. There can be great pleasure in discovering your pieces/furnishings along the way. I love making purchases while traveling. It brings home the vacation experience and also brings added pleasure to the organic hunt of finding what you like and how it will work in your space.

Sound advice to keep in your mental arsenal, which you should have stocked just as amply as your household toolbox, battery drawer and first-aid kit!

Welcome to My Neighborhood: A Mini Tour of Harlem with Author/Historian Jim Mackin

―――――――

I first met my neighbor Jim Mackin right in the middle of the pandemic. I'd read an article that he'd written a new book, *Notable New Yorkers of Manhattan's Upper West Side,* and that he would be appearing around the corner at his favorite pastry shop where he would be outside signing and selling copies. I thought that was an ingenious way to host a book release party and you would even get a free croissant and coffee with every purchase!

Jim had been a sought-after tour guide before the lockdown, so the book is a wonderful tool to give yourself a walking tour of the area and find out some fascinating hidden history about famous residents like Humphrey Bogart, Billie Holiday, Amelia Earhart, Yul Brynner, Barack Obama, Maya Angelou and Gloria Swanson. I masked up and bundled myself against the winter chill and set out to get my copy. Jim and I quickly discovered we not only had a shared interest in local neighborhood history but also music, ranging from the *Great American Songbook* and Broadway to the more obscure vaudevillian specialty numbers of the early Twentieth Century. And, like me, he was a marathon runner. Once we had been introduced, we started literally running into each other on our morning miles along Riverside Drive.

It's a joy to take a walk around a New York City neighborhood with Jim, because he can expose the ghosts on almost any corner! Over the last century, Harlem has evolved from predominantly Italian and Jewish enclaves to Latino and African American communities and these days, the current renaissance with Columbia University's expansion into the Manhattanville neighborhood has made it even more of a melting pot.

The building where I live stands where there had originally been a Vaudeville, then silent-movie theater, built in 1902. Decades later it became a Baptist church before falling into disrepair and was razed. Most visitors to Harlem gravitate to the famed Apollo Theater on 125th Street, where some of the greatest artists past and present have performed: Duke Ellington, Sammy Davis Jr, Jimi Hendrix, Diana Ross, Louis Armstrong and countless others. (I got to memorably interview the late Chadwick Boseman on the stage of the Apollo back in 2014 when he was playing Little Richard in the bio pic *Get On Up*.). I thought it might be fun to have Jim take us, on these pages, on a virtual walk around Harlem to give you some backstory on the area. If you make a visit to Harlem someday, you'll enjoy visiting some of these sites in addition to all the other wonderful restaurants, shops and cultural locations.

From Jim:

Who knows what's in the hood—the hood being the neighborhood known as Morningside Heights, bordering on Harlem, bordering on

Manhattanville. So much history, so much culture, so many surprises. Thurgood Marshall and Amelia Earhart once lived nearby. So did Harry Houdini. These and many other interesting residents and their addresses can be found in my book, *Notable New Yorker's of Manhattan's Upper West Side: Bloomingdale and Morningside Heights.*

Because the area was so far north of the city until the late 1880s, the Dutch called it Bloemendael, which meant "blooming dale, or vale," and it was Anglicized over time to Bloomingdale. Parts were named the Plains of Harlem, Vanderwater Heights, Harlem Heights, and Morningside Heights. The Battle of Harlem Heights in 1776 was key to colonial history, but the Bloomingdale Insane Asylum put the area on the map when it opened in 1821. It established the area's institutional character and harbored the Leake and Watts Orphanage, St. Luke's and Sydenham Hospitals, Columbia University and Barnard and Teachers Colleges, Union Theological and Jewish Theological Seminaries, Riverside Church and the Cathedral of St. John the Divine, and numerous other social establishments.

The Ninth Avenue elevated subway, from 1878, and the Interborough Rapid Transit underground subway, from 1904, populated the area big time. A few more notables who lived in the area:

Rube Goldberg, the cartoonist and namesake of complicated contraptions, Ruth Bader Ginsberg, Associate Justice of the Supreme Court, affectionately known as RBG,

George Carlin, the irreverent comedian,
Oscar Hammerstein II, Lyricist of *Showboat, Oklahoma, Carousel,*
The King and I and *The Sound of Music*
Henry Luce, the co-founder of *Time* magazine,
Daniel Tiemann, Mayor of New York City when Central Park was begun,
Albert Von Tilzer, who wrote *Take Me Out to the Ballgame.*

Just two blocks away is the world-famous Apollo theater which helped
launch the careers of Billie Holiday, Sarah Vaughn, Diana Ross and the
Supremes, James Brown, Aretha Franklin, the Jackson Five including
Michael Jackson, Stevie Wonder, and many others. The Apollo lobby is a
museum of African American musical history, and Wednesday's Amateur
Night is not to be missed.

A short walk north on Convent Avenue brings you past the long-gone
Manhattanville College Campus to the elegant campus of the City College
of New York. A short walk west will take you to Columbia University's
modern campus addition and a delightful park along the Hudson River.
It was here that in 1865 the train carrying Lincoln's body slowed for silent
acknowledgement by the inhabitants of Manhattanville.

No street in the middle of all these has more style than Hancock Place. The
hero of the Battle of Gettysburg, General Winifred Scott Hancock, lost the
election for President of the United States in 1880 to James Garfield by less
than forty thousand votes. Hancock Park on Hancock Place with Hancock's

bust is most appropriate given his final public role in presiding over the funeral of President Grant in 1885 nearby, at what would become the largest mausoleum in the country and known as Grant's Tomb.

The hood is never static. It never shuts down. Restaurants and 24-hour deliveries feed its dynamic populous as its deep and rich history feeds the hood to make more notables and enrich its very special character.

Note from Author: Manhattan's ever-changing restaurant scene is renowned, especially as Covid raged, but it's safe to bet that when you make a visit to Harlem, you'll want to check out stalwart establishments like Melba's (one of Prince Harry and Meghan's favorites) and Red Rooster, as well as newer contemporary classics like Clay, Vinateria and the more casual but no less spectacular Silvana.

At-Home Workout with Strength Mate Fitness CEO, Mark Dancewicz

---

I have been an avid gym goer and fitness enthusiast my entire adult life and, as I mentioned previously, if it hadn't been for my work as an aerobics instructor, I might never have parlayed that into a broadcast career that has spanned decades! (Adaptability and a willingness to try new things are qualities that work in most aspects of life). For many years prior to 2020, I had a regimented routine of running three or four days a week and hitting the gym with a personal trainer twice weekly. Even when traveling for work, as I was doing almost weekly before the pandemic, I was a fixture at the hotel gyms, whether it was a four a.m. jet lag treadmill run in Tokyo, a shipboard session sailing to the Great Barrier Reef or cowering in a corner of the Beverly Hills Equinox while watching in amazement at the workouts of Chris Hemsworth, Antonio Banderas or Dwayne Johnson.

But when our gyms closed, we had to find ways to adapt. For the ten weeks of quarantine I spent in the Hamptons, I was lucky enough to have a home gym available to me, but after that there were adjustments to be made. My Facetime trainer, Johnny D, recommended a brand of elastic bands and that got me through many months of muscle toning. I also feel like the Age of Covid turned me into a better, heartier runner because it forced me to log my miles outside, regardless of the weather. When it was

90 degrees with subtropical humidity or below freezing with snowbanks, it would have been much easier to jump on a health club's cardio machine. I didn't have that option.

While my new apartment building does have an excellent gym for residents, being able to facilitate workouts within your own home has grown in popularity so much that it has, for millions, become the new norm. We all remember the era when Soloflex multi-purpose weight machines were in everyone's garage or den, usually used more as clothes trees than for muscle-building. Almost nothing makes me more uncomfortable than seeing some huge piece of cardiovascular equipment like a treadmill, Peleton bike, rowing machine or StairMaster dominating an otherwise comfortable family room. Figure out a way to designate or cordon off your gymnasium area. And, wherever that is, make absolutely sure it is kept clean, hygienic and odor-free.

I asked my own personal trainer, Mark Dancewicz of Strength Mate Fitness, for some advice on outfitting myself for home workouts and wanted to share what he's taught me, as well as some useful ideas you can try for yourself. Of course, it is always recommended that you consult with your personal health care provider before beginning any new exercise program.

Nelson: What adjustments did you have to make when gyms started closing and Covid protocols went into place?

Mark: I trained clients virtually even before the Pandemic. Exercise is a very personal journey, and some people find they like the convenience and privacy of their own home. When the Pandemic hit I think everyone was confused on how long it was going to last and when we realized what we were facing, all sporting goods and exercise equipment flew off the shelves. As a trainer, this gave me the opportunity to get very creative with workouts. I think people's main concern with working out virtually is whether or not their workouts will be as productive and efficient.

Nelson: They can be, providing the motivation is there, right?

Mark: Right! The mental benefit of exercise is just as important as the physical. I think once my clients realized we could achieve the same goals previously set by incorporating body weight and household objects, they began to find a new sense of accomplishment. That, to me, was exciting. A good trainer will consistently change up your routine to keep the body guessing. This was the perfect opportunity.

Nelson: Bad news for the gym franchises. Now a lot of people prefer working out from home.

Mark: The beauty of exercise is that it can be accomplished in the smallest of spaces.

Nelson: How should folks prepare to get started on a new/at-home fitness program? Of course, one should consult with their doctor before beginning or altering an exercise regimen.

Mark: The most important take-away for anyone beginning their fitness journey or tackling a new routine is that there is only one you. You are unique, therefore your muscle imbalances are unique. What are muscle imbalances? The easiest way to describe this is if muscles on one side of a joint become too tight from overuse, it could cause the muscles on the other side to become too weak from lack of use. Muscles become imbalanced from everyday circumstances. Sitting at a desk all day looking down at a computer or your phone, walking in high heels, picking up your children and positioning them on one hip or even just carrying your purse or backpack. We all have them. Work with a trainer to identify and expose your imbalances through a body assessment, then the exercises and stretches you should be doing to correct them. It's the best way to ensure that you are starting from the safest place.

Nelson: What would be a standard assessment you'd give?

Mark: A routine assessment I put all new clients through: 45 jumping jacks, 45 high knees, 10 squats, 10 jump squats, 6-8 pushups, a 60-second plank, 45 mountain climbers and 10 lunges. Through these exercises I can gauge a person's endurance, flexibility, and core strength, as well as expose muscle imbalances. This whole routine can be done in your living room, bedroom or even hotel room. Here is a fun test for you. Try some of these exercises but place your keys or a quarter on the floor next to you. Following the completion of 45 jumping jacks and 45 high knees, look down. Did you move away from the keys or quarter? If the answer is yes, your stabilization and balance are off due to lack of core strength. Work on your planks! So, after we expose imbalances, now the fun begins!

Nelson: I ate an awful lot of lasagna and other comfort foods during lockdown! Everybody was laughing about the Covid 19-pound weight gain!

Mark: You can have any body you want; you just need to put in the work. Set small, attainable goals! What do you want to accomplish? Weight loss, toning and sculpting, or maybe just flexibility and agility.

Nelson: What would you say is the very basic equipment to have at home?

Mark: Equipment is going to differ depending on your goals. Dumbbells of varying weights are going to be the most beneficial for your at home gym. There are many adjustable dumbbells on the market that would be a great investment. Whether it is sculpting and toning your triceps or building up your chest, having weight is going to advance any exercise. Resistance bands are an incredible way to cut, tone, recruit stabilization muscles and burn fat. Fold them up and throw them in a drawer. These bad boys are key and will help you attain a great sweat!

Nelson: The cheap bands snap and break easily. I finally spent a few extra bucks and got a good set that seem to last through anything.

Mark: Working on a hardwood floor can be harsh on knees and lower back during an Ab series, which you always should be doing. Strengthening your core is the most important part of any routine; it's where your power comes from. So, I always have a rolled-up yoga mat nearby.

Nelson: I do not want to see a rowing machine in the house! What about cardio?

Mark: Jump rope, my friend! Jumping rope along with resistance band training is the best way to lose extra pounds. But if you do find yourself with a little space, getting a collapsible workout bench is a game changer. Fold it up and put it under the bed or in a closet. This staple will assure that you get a well-rounded routine. But the most important equipment is footwear. Good sneakers with great support are essential. Remember those muscle imbalances I was speaking of? Old sneakers with worn-out soles will cause/exacerbate muscle imbalances.

Nelson: I am a pronator, so I understand that! I alternate two pairs of running shoes and relegate them to simply walking around the neighborhood after they get four hundred miles on them. For me, the hardest part about working out at home is getting/staying motivated. I try to experiment with new things like yoga or Pilates, but I admit to getting stuck in my ways.

Mark: Fitness is a lifestyle. There will always be goals to achieve and because of that your routine or focus might change. Start safe and simple, listen to your body. One of the most common things I hear from people is that they are bored. That just means it's time to switch things up. Get excited! A new piece of equipment will always get me pumped and before you know it you have built yourself a nice little gym. It's your space and everything in it is a trophy that you have earned along the way. It is a reminder of the hours you spent sweating, the negative thoughts and insecurities you overcame, and the push, drive, and action you chose to better yourself.

Nelson: Where do you suggest finding a virtual trainer?

Mark: Somehow, we always hear of a great doctor, therapist, or hairdresser through our friends, so I would start there! My clients have brought me many people over the years, and I find a recommendation to be the highest compliment. Next, check out their websites or social media! It is a great way to see personality and what they have to offer. A great physique will always get your attention but there are many other important things you should be looking for when consulting with a trainer. Your trainer should hold a certification from a credible organization, (NASM, ACE, ISSA, AFFA etc.) and have personal experience outside their certification. Having been a Broadway dancer, I spent hours training in and out of the gym. In addition, ballet, yoga, and swimming helped build the stamina it took to perform eight shows a week.

I found that this background and the knowledge I gained from having examined my own body over the years helped provide me with tools to communicate proper form to a client. Every trainer is going to have a different approach when it comes to explaining what muscles you have to engage on the inside of the body to get the correct form on the outside. I work with analogies. I find using everyday circumstances are something we can all relate to. Your trainer should ask you questions about preexisting conditions, past injuries, likes and dislikes and what goals you are trying to accomplish. A great trainer will put you at ease. I explain to every new client that, "this is a partnership, a team effort, you and me. I will go through this with you every step of the way and my success is determined by your success."

Nelson: It can't hurt to give it a try!

Mark: Absolutely. After a few sessions I would ask myself, do I have fun with this trainer? Do I look forward to our workouts? Do I trust him/her? Do I trust him/her enough to fill them in on all the insecurities I have when it comes to exercise, food, alcohol and lack of drive. If the answer is yes, then I think you found a great trainer. And most trainers these days offer a virtual option.

Nelson: What about YouTube videos?

Mark: I am not a fan of using YouTube clips during your actual session. If you want to search for videos to get ideas on new exercises, I applaud you for you dedication and research. But when you are actually working out, you can't focus on your form or alignment if your head is turned to the side looking at a screen. The difference between YouTube tutorials and a virtual session is that your trainer is watching your form and giving you vocal cues to correct alignment during the exercise.

When I was a young trainer, I adopted the motto, "bodies in motion STAY in motion." To me, mobility unlocks all your other potential. Having seen many of my relatives age well into their nineties, I am witness to the truth of using it, or risk losing it! Treasure and maintain your wellness to the best of your ability because a healthy home is a happy home. My wish is that you've found some inspiration in these pages to make your "castle" just such a place—physically, psychologically and spiritually. Let me know how it goes!

—Nelson

Acknowledgments

An enormous thank you to my editor, Charlene Keel, a pal from thirty years ago with whom I reconnected following the unexpected death of our dear mutual friend, Philece Sampler. Philece was one of those bright lights of love and energy who had a knack for bringing people together — something she managed to do even after leaving this world. This book wouldn't exist without her.

Many thanks to Micky Hyman, CEO at Red Sky Entertainment.

Gratitude to incredible Rebecca Roberts of Method & Moxie. Not only did she commandeer the titanic task of being our Interior Designer, she project managed everything from start to finish with the patience, calmness, confidence and grace that Jonny and I could never have mustered on our own. She became a life coach and friend.

Garrett Rowland's interior photos are treasure for which we are most grateful.

Thanks to all the talented designers, doctors, developers and insightful colleagues who helped add color with their perspectives, tips and tricks. "It takes a village," but never more so than when compiling a book, and it gives me a warm feeling to be able to include so many folks whose expertise and perspective mean a lot to me.

Made in the USA
Middletown, DE
07 January 2023

21569288R00097